What You Can Do RIGHT NOW to Help Your Child with Autism

Jonathan Levy

SOURCEBOOKS, INC.
NAPERVILLE, ILLINOIS

This publication is designed to provide accurate and authoritative information in regard to the subject matter covered. It is sold with the understanding that the publisher is not engaged in rendering legal, accounting, or other professional service. If legal advice or other expert assistance is required, the services of a competent professional person should be sought.—*From a Declaration of Principles Jointly Adopted by a Committee of the American Bar Association and a Committee of Publishers and Associations*

This book is not intended as a substitute for medical advice from a qualified physician. The intent of this book is to provide accurate general information in regard to the subject matter covered. If medical advice or other expert help is needed, the services of an appropriate medical professional should be sought.

All brand names and product names used in this book are trademarks, registered trademarks, or trade names of their respective holders. Sourcebooks, Inc., is not associated with any product or vendor in this book.

Published by Sourcebooks, Inc.
P.O. Box 4410, Naperville, Illinois 60567-4410
(630) 961-3900
Fax: (630) 961-2168
www.sourcebooks.com

Library of Congress Cataloging-in-Publication Data

Levy, Jonathan, 1971 Oct. 31-
    10 things you can do right now to help your child with autism / Jonathan Levy.
        p. cm.
    Includes index.
    1. Autism in children. 2. Autistic children--Family relationships. 3. Parents of autistic children. I. Title. II. Title: Ten things you can do right now to help your child with autism.

RJ506.A9L4845 2007
618.92'85882--dc22

2006100619

Printed and bound in the United States of America.
RRD 10 9 8 7 6 5

Contents

Dedication

This is for the parents and their sweet children,
and everyone else who touches their lives.

Acknowledgments

I'd like to thank Steve and Andrew, who encouraged me to write this book one warm summer day.

My mother, for saying, "Can I show this to my editor?" Also, for the whole carrying me for nine months thing.

My father, for reading the first draft in one day.

Bears and Samahria, without whom my life would be completely different.

Raun, for being my friend.

Daniel Markowitz and Erika Schuler for their medical expertise.

Bryn, Kate, William, Suzanne, Gerd, and Steven, for teaching me along the way.

Carly, Eric, Dave and Rebecca, Adam, Aaron and Kris, and Dawn for the continued support.

Preface

I learned the techniques outlined in this book at the Autism Treatment Center of America (ATCA) in Sheffield, Massachusetts. The center, founded by Barry Neil Kaufman and Samahria Lyte Kaufman, first opened in 1983, after the Kaufmans were deluged with interest from parents of children with autism who had read their bestselling book *Son-Rise* or watched the NBC movie of the week about their work with their son Raun.

Raun Kaufman was diagnosed as severely autistic in the early 1970s, with a tested IQ under 40. Barry and Samahria were told to institutionalize Raun, but instead they invented a new way of working with someone with autism. Their techniques were revolutionary and produced a revolutionary result: Raun completely emerged from autism, graduated from college, and went on to live a life with friends, girlfriends, and all the normal trappings. Raun, whom I met while working as a staff member at the center, remains one of my best friends and has no vestiges of autism.

I first ventured to the center in 1993 and joined the staff in early 1994. I underwent a (sometimes grueling) three-and-a-half-year training program there, at the end of which I graduated and ultimately became a senior staff member and teacher. In 2000 I left to set up a private practice, which continues to this day.

The approach the Kaufmans invented, the Son-Rise Program®, is much more involved than what is described in this book. This book is a collection of the most valuable techniques from that program that can quickly be put into practice.

Much gratitude to Barry and Samahria, both for creating an approach that has helped so many families, and because without them, I would have never met their son, and my life would be poorer for it.

Why You Should Listen

I've been bitten, spit at, and vomited on. I've had tables thrown at me and I've been urinated on.

I've also been hugged by children who won't let other people touch them. I've played for an hour with a child who had never played with anyone for more than five minutes. I've helped children from all over the world—even the ones who bit me, spat at me, and threw heavy objects at me—say their first words.

I've seen parents thank me, question me, yell with frustration, cry with gratitude, sob with sadness, and fight with each other. I know what parents want: a clear way to help their child.

I wrote this book so you, the parent (or grandparent, friend, teacher, or anyone else who is involved) of a child with autism could have some easily accessible techniques that I *know* work with the vast majority of kids with autism. Some of these techniques are considered controversial; some are not.

I've taught and demonstrated these techniques to over a thousand parents in the United States, England, Denmark, the Netherlands, France, Canada, and Trinidad. Most of the teaching has been done in one-on-one settings, though I have also taught seminars and was one of the autism experts featured in the BBC documentary *I Want My Little Boy Back*. I have lectured in many places, from a tiny basement in Iowa to a hospital in Denmark. I have been an expert witness on autism at a due process hearing.

I also have had the opportunity to work with approximately eight hundred children with autism one-on-one in those twelve years. It is hard to calculate precisely, but it is not stretching to say that I have spent over twenty-five hundred hours working one-on-one with these children.

If you do just some of the ten things I recommend, you will almost certainly see results over time. In all my years of working with families, I can only think of three families who really did what I taught them and didn't see changes in their child.

I ask that you read this book with an open mind and heart. If there is advice or activities in the book that you don't agree with, don't do them. Understand, though, that everything here is my best advice to you. If you don't understand or agree with a topic or chapter, be open to the possibility that there could be something useful in there.

Finally, I invite you to have fun as you read this. I know that people take autism very seriously, and for good reason. But I believe there is virtue in trying to talk about it and not having it be so heavy and so tragic. I am hopeful that this book can make a difference in the lives of both you and your child. I believe it can. In fact, I believe it will. All you have to do is turn the page...

The 10 Things

1. Don't react
2. Make eye contact a priority
3. Join with the stims
4. Respond differently to crying
5. Give your child as much control as possible
6. Focus on your attitude
7. Work one-on-one in a non-distracting room
8. Be dynamic with your child
9. Get more language
10. Make sure food isn't part of the problem

A Few Other Things You Should Know

How to Think about Autism

Autism is a disorder that has many symptoms:

   Many autistic children do not speak easily.
   Some do not speak at all.
   Some do not use utensils when they eat.
   Some are not potty-trained.
   Some have motor challenges.

All autistic children have ways of dropping into their own worlds, leaving us behind for a minute, an hour, a day.

This is the essence of autism: a disorder that is, at its heart, about interaction. Most of the symptoms come from either a lack of paying attention to other people or a lack of interest in joining in with the rest of the world.

Because this is the case, it is important that when you work with your child, you address the core issue of autism: your child, for one reason or another, is not spending enough time in our interactive world. That's what you most want to be dealing with, instead of issues like reading and spelling.

This book addresses issues of speech and crying and many other things, but all my advice comes from a very particular goal: to help your child interact more deeply and consistently. Everything else is easier to teach as your child becomes more interactive.

About the Intensive Program at the Autism Treatment Center of America

I am going to refer to a particular program at ATCA called the Son-Rise Program Intensive throughout this book, so here's a quick synopsis of what it is.

My main position at the center involved me as a family trainer in the intensive program.

The Son-Rise Program Intensive is a five-day treatment program. A family would come on Sunday night and stay through the following Friday evening. Over the course of the week, the staff works one-on-one with the child in a specialized playroom designed to help the child learn faster. The child facilitators work with the child each day from 9:00 a.m. to 5:00 p.m. Family trainers observe the parents working with their child and then teach them how to be more effective.

The families would stay in an apartment for the week. The specialized playroom was in the apartment so the family could use it with their child after the day had ended.

I started out as a facilitator-in-training and worked my way to being a trainer. Eventually, I even got to train trainers.

About the Stories
All of the stories contained in this book are true. The names of the parents and children have been changed to protect their privacy.

#1

Don't React

*How you do and don't respond
makes all the difference*

About Bobby

In 1995, a family came to ATCA with their five-year-old autistic son. Bobby had many challenges that most autistic children share: he did not speak, he made fleeting eye contact, and he focused more on objects than people. But there was another thing about Bobby, one that separated him from any other child I have ever seen or worked with: he vomited all the time.

When Bobby came to a two-week version of the intensive program, he was vomiting forty times per day. This is not an exaggeration. He literally vomited almost three times per hour. Although we had never seen anything like this before, there seemed to be only a few possible explanations. After working with Bobby for nine days, he made clear progress. I still remember leaving the playroom at the end of the day on a Tuesday afternoon. I looked at the "vomit chart" we used to keep track of his throwing up, and saw he hadn't vomited once all day. I mentioned this to his mother, Sarah, and she told me, astonishingly, that it was the first day since he was one year old that he hadn't vomited!

Four years of nearly constant vomiting, and just a few days into his intensive program, Bobby had changed dramatically. How could this have happened, and so quickly?

You're a Cartoon Character

Reactions are the cues we give to our children right after they do something. Sometimes a reaction is a celebration; sometimes it is an admonishment. Either way, what you do directly after your child has done something—positive or negative—has a direct impact on the frequency and intensity of him doing that action again. For example, if an autistic child knocks over a glass and milk spills on the carpet, many parents will yell at him, or at least express some form of frustration. It's viewed by most as normal parenting. Ironically enough, this type of response to the spilled milk encourages your child to spill the milk in the future! Sounds crazy, right? It does to most people the first time they hear it. But if you allow yourself to look more closely at the situation from the child's perspective, it makes perfect sense.

Many times, autistic children do not have much control in their lives. They are dressed by an adult, told to sit (and stay sitting) at a desk, given foods chosen by adults, etc. There's not very much children can do to make the adults around them act as they want. However, sometimes they do something (often by accident) that an adult reacts to in a big and entertaining way, like yelling. Most of the time, these reactions are of a negative nature. Think about it: how often do you *celebrate* your child in a loud way? Now compare that to how often you yell or make an intense face at your child when he has done something you don't approve of. In many cases, we reserve our loudest and biggest reactions for the negative stuff. Now, imagine you are an autistic child who doesn't have much control over the world around you. Suddenly you spill some milk. Your mother makes a face or yells or just changes in some way (perhaps because she's annoyed). You just created that reaction! All you had to do was push a glass over and your mother changed instantly. And she looked so funny! Remember, kids love cartoons. They think it's funny when they see Wile E. Coyote scream when an anvil lands on his foot. Now, suddenly, you're reacting like the cartoon character. And all the child has to do to get this fun response from you again is spill some more milk. That's easy enough to do.

How You Respond

Make a list, using this chart, of the things your child does that you wish he would stop and how you respond to the behavior (in the "your external reaction" column). In the "rating" column, write a number from one to ten rating how big/loud/intense your response is. Ten is a huge response, and one suggests you're in a coma.

Your child's behavior	Your external reaction	Rating
Hitting his sister	I picked him up and said "no."	7

Look at all the behaviors that you give interesting and/or entertaining reactions to. These are behaviors that you might be able to help your child change just by changing how you react to them. Pretty cool, huh?

I Know What *Not* to Do. But What Do I Do Instead?

This part is both easy and difficult. You basically want to give your child the impression that whatever it is that she's just done has not affected your world. So in the case of the child who spilled the milk, you'd want to be very nonchalant. It's no big deal to you. You're not upset. You just slowly and calmly clean up the spill. If your response is not interesting, your child is much less likely to repeat the behavior.

Of course, there are behaviors a child with autism does just because they fascinate him. Your reaction is not nearly as much of a motivating factor in this case, though you could encourage one of these behaviors to occur even more often by having a strong negative reaction. For example, a child may flush a toilet repeatedly because he loves to see the water *whoosh*. If a parent yells at the child for the constant flushing, the child now might flush for two reasons: he loves the whooshing *and* he gets the reaction.

Remember Bobby, the vomiter, from the beginning of the chapter? His mother, as it turned out, was a neat freak. She told us how she would polish a doorknob in her home and then yell at her (nonautistic) daughter for opening the door and getting fingerprints on the doorknob. So Bobby found the thing that got his mother the most upset of all: vomiting. Everywhere. All the time.

Sometimes people ask how it was physically possible that Bobby could vomit so often. First of all, he didn't often vomit very much (when you vomit every twenty minutes, there just isn't that much left in your stomach sometimes), and when he would take a drink, it was a near certainty that it was coming back up a few minutes later. Bobby was constantly requesting water so he could then vomit it back up.

Our staff spent a lot of time with Bobby, cleaning up his vomit without giving a big reaction to it. That may sound challenging, but it really wasn't. Once I knew that the vomit was coming, I began to see getting vomited on as part of my job. This is similar to how parents respond when an infant spits up. It's messy, but you knew it was going to happen, and many parents don't have any reaction to it at all. It's just part of the job of being a parent. It was the same thing here (only with a lot more liquid).

Deciding It's Okay

The best and easiest way to learn to not react to the things your child does is to decide that it is okay that your child does them. I know you probably react precisely because you *don't* think it's okay that your child does these behaviors. However, your judging these behaviors as bad or inappropriate is not helping the situation. If anything, it's fueling your child's interest in doing these behaviors. So, right now, stop. Take a deep breath. Look at the chart from earlier in the chapter. Picture one of these behaviors in your mind. Be open to the idea that it's okay that your child does this behavior, even though there may be things about it that make your life more challenging. Decide that it's okay if your child does this. It's happened many times before; it's probably going to happen many times again. So you might as well decide it's okay.

This doesn't mean that you won't clean up the milk or catch the vase your child has just thrown before it hits the ground. I am only referring to your internal emotional response. The more you can feel at peace with your child's behaviors, the easier it will be for you to give a reaction of nonchalance when your child does one of the things that's on your list.

Dennis

One time a family came to ATCA with concerns about how their child would interact with new people. According to his parents, Dennis hit new people repeatedly and then he'd cry and scream. I happened to be the first one with Dennis on his first day. Although it was not the way we normally did things, his mother insisted on staying in the room during the first meeting of myself and Dennis, to help him get acclimated. I can still remember the three of us sitting in the playroom, playing a board game, when Dennis crawled over to me. I was about to roll the dice when he looked in my eyes and hit me lightly on the thigh. His mother made a face of disapproval and concern, but she was behind him, so Dennis didn't see her. Instead, he watched to see how I would react to his slap.

I continued smiling and rolled the dice. Inside, I felt fine as well. His hit wasn't painful. I had known something like this was going to happen. I also knew that having any kind of a big reaction to the hit would only encourage him to continue to hit me.

Dennis's eyes moved from mine to following the roll of the dice. He announced that I had rolled a five, and moved my game piece accordingly. His mother's face transformed from concern to looking pleased. She stayed with us for another few minutes and then left. Dennis did not hit me anymore. Nor did he hit any of the other staff members, nor cry or scream for his mother at any time during the week.

What happened with Dennis was extremely common. Children are constantly giving us tests, observing our reactions, and behaving accordingly.

The Other Half

So now you know about how to discourage some of your child's behaviors. Of course, there are some things your child does that you want him to keep doing. How do you encourage those behaviors?

Let's start by filling in another chart. This time, write about behaviors your child does that you wish he did more of. Include how you react to these behaviors, as well as a rating from one to ten based on the volume/intensity/size of your reaction.

Your child's behavior	Your external reaction	Rating
Playing gently with the dog	A smile, sometimes	2

Compare your ratings (the 1–10 you filled out for each reaction) to the ratings from the first chart in this chapter. If you are like most people, your numbers were higher on the first chart. This is because we've been taught that good parenting often involves keeping your child in the dark when he's doing something you'd want him to do. The assumption is that he'll notice it and then stop doing it right away.

In fact, children (and adults) respond to celebration by doing more of the behavior they were celebrated for. Any time we give a big response, people pretty much do more of what they were doing. When we give small (or no) responses, people generally do less of what they were doing. You'll probably be surprised at how much your reactions encourage or discourage behavior.

Saying things like, "That was great!" with a big smile on your face and a lot of enthusiasm really does make a difference. Of course, you have to actually feel that something was great to have any real impact on your child. Kids with autism have incredible radar for sincerity.

It has always fascinated me that basic parenting involves having big negative reactions for the behaviors we want to discourage and relatively small positive reactions to the behaviors we want to encourage, because this is exactly the opposite of what works. There are some children who respond differently than this—some kids will stop doing a behavior as soon as you celebrate it. If your child is like this, then tone down your celebrations to whatever extent is necessary. You might say quietly, "Nice job" or "Well done."

To Review:

- How you react to your child's behaviors has a direct impact on whether your child repeats those behaviors.
- Be nonchalant about the things you want to discourage.

- Celebrate what you want to encourage.
- Both your internal (how you feel) and external (what you do) reactions count.
- If you don't judge your child's behaviors, it is much easier to not give a reaction.

#2

Make Eye Contact
a Priority

*The key to helping your child form
deeper relationships*

The Issue with Jimmy

Jimmy was a six-year-old boy I had worked with
several times over the past two years. He had
improved tremendously, going from no language to
literally thousands of words. It was like he had been
paying attention for all those years he was nonverbal—listening, thinking, learning, but with no way
to get the words out. It seemed he had all those
words in there, waiting until he could figure out how
to say them. His family started the program and his
language avalanched.

His family had brought him back to ATCA for
more training. I was the first to work with him this
time. In the playroom, we drew a huge picture of
Superman, and Jimmy asked me what it would be like

to fly. I was struck by how much he had changed. We were having a fascinating conversation! And yet something was gnawing at me. Something was off. His parents watched me working with him, and when I came out of the room, they rushed up to me, excited about the session and how far Jimmy had come. I agreed with them, and went off to lunch, still unsure about what was wrong. Then it hit me: Jimmy had barely looked at me during our hour-long session.

The Most Intimate Thing in the World

Autism is, at its core, a disorder that impairs interaction. Although some children with autism speak and some don't, some use the potty and some don't, and some can participate in an academic setting and some can't, all of them fundamentally have difficulties interacting with other people.

The most direct—and most intimate—way we interact meaningfully with each other is through eye contact. Eye contact forces our attention to be on the person we are looking at.

We know that people with autism remove themselves from our world. So it makes sense that they have poor eye contact. If they looked other people in the eyes regularly, they'd be interacting more, and that is exactly what they are trying to avoid.

The More They Look, the More They Learn

The thing about eye contact is that everybody wants to put it on the back burner. Most parents believe that eye contact is not as important as learning speech, social skills, or even potty training. But the thing is, we get a huge chunk of our information about the world from what we see. Infants, for example, have remarkable eye contact. Babies are fascinated by people; they want to interact with us, they look into our eyes, and that's why they learn so much so fast.

If you want your child to learn faster, then you have to help your child look more. Speech, social skills, potty training—everything goes faster when you have improved eye contact.

If your child is watching you closely, then of course he is going to learn how to speak better. He is watching how you form the words. He is noticing all the subtleties of language and interaction that we couldn't explain if we tried. You are a model of how to be in the world. If your child is watching you, your child is learning from you. We had a saying in ATCA: the more they look, the more they learn.

My Child Has Good Eye Contact

Improving eye contact is vital to your child's learning to be with other people in meaningful ways. Sometimes parents focus on some of the other challenges that face children with autism and deprioritize eye contact. In some ways this is understandable: how do you really help your child to look more? It seems hard. Besides (many parents say), my child has good eye contact.

Stop.

No, he doesn't.

No, they say. *My* child really does have good eye contact.

Trust me. He doesn't.

The odds are your child needs to work on his eye contact more than any other skill. Certainly there are exceptions to this. But a good 98 percent of you need to take this in: you must help your child to look more. This is top priority.

My Cousin

I went to a family function in Ohio a number of years ago. My grandparents introduced me to Sally and Fred. Sally and Fred had a child with autism. Sally was a fourth cousin twice removed, so I had never met them before. They explained to me that

Sam, their autistic son, was twenty-eight and had a job. I was delighted to hear that he had done so well for himself.

Fred confided in me that they wished Sam had more social skills, but he lived by himself, drove a car, and did fine. I asked to meet Sam. Sally looked around the room and didn't see him anywhere.

Then I had a thought. I went down to the basement. Sitting on the couch, watching TV, was a lone man.

"I'm Jonathan," I said.

"I'm Sam." He said this while still looking at the TV.

Sam and I proceeded to have a fifteen-minute conversation about his life. I asked him many questions, and he answered them all. He did not look at me during the entire conversation, save once. That was when I said to him, "Could you look at me, Sam?"

He did for the briefest of moments. Then his eyes darted back to the television.

Sam is absolutely a success story. He has a job, he can drive, and he lives by himself. I know many of you would give your right arm for your child to have these things. But before you go amputating any body parts, it's important to note that there are also some things Sam didn't have, but could have had (with the right help):

- A girlfriend
- A best friend
- Any friends at all
- The ability to make friends

Once you get past basic survival issues, many of the most precious things that we want in life involve how we relate to other people. *The relationships that form our lives are how we define ourselves.* And relationships are the most important thing in almost everybody's life.

Charting Eye Contact

It's important to get a strong sense of where your child's eye contact really is. Take the following chart and start observing your child in the same room with another person. Ask the person to do their best to play with your child. Observe for five minutes. Put a check mark in the chart every time your child looks at the other person *in the eyes.* Got that? Not in the chest or in their general direction, but actually in the other person's eyes. That's all that counts.

Charting Eye Contact

Date	Who your child played with	Looks

I included some extra rows so you could do this more than once.

Now, let's score the numbers:

No. of looks	What it means
0–5	You gotta get working on this.
6–10	Really, you gotta get on this.
11–15	Not too shabby. But still, this is a top priority for your child.
15–20	Your child is looking 3–4 times per minute. Pretty good. Not enough.
21–30	This is good eye contact. Even this needs to be worked on some.
31+	Fine. You were right and I was wrong.

There are two factors that are not captured in this chart: duration and spontaneity. Your child could look only seven times over the five minutes but look for so long each time that it's clear he has impressive eye contact. Spontaneity is the difference between a child looking based on his initiative versus someone else initiating it. Ideally, you'd want your child to look of his own accord, but this is often something that has to be worked on.

Watch Out for the Kids Who Talk

Jimmy, the boy from the beginning of the chapter, had learned to speak in conversational sentences. He spoke so much that everyone got caught up in having meaningful and educational conversations with him, and it pulled us away from working on eye contact with him. This happens all the time when children acquire speech skills: everyone gets so focused on talking that they assume the eye contact is there. If your child is talking to you, that's wonderful! Make sure he's looking, too.

After my session, the staff renewed our goal to help Jimmy with his eye contact. It improved quickly and he is in a regular school today, with no vestiges of autism. He has friends, and he knows how to make more.

Techniques to Improve Eye Contact

Now that you know why eye contact is so important, here's what you do to get more of it.

Positioning

Positioning is vital to encouraging eye contact. Sit in a chair and have a friend stand in front of you. Make eye contact with your friend when she is standing up. Note how this feels in your eye muscles. Now have your friend kneel down and be at or slightly below your eye level. Note how your eyes feel.

See the difference? Looking up creates a fair amount of strain on your eyes. Looking at or below your eye level is no strain at all. You want it to be easy for your child to look at you.

Another aspect of positioning is making sure you are in your child's line of sight. This means you do not want to be behind your child or to your child's side. Instead, you want to be in front of your child whenever possible.

Put the Batman Up to Your Nose

Children with autism look at a lot of things, just not people. Mainly, they look at what they're interested in. If you have a potato chip and give it to your child, chances are your child will look right at that chip. It makes sense because he needs to know where to reach for it. This is true for pretty much anything you give to your child (that he wants).

There are some children who are so deeply absorbed in their repetitive behaviors that they don't look up at the object at all, instead reaching out (with almost a sixth sense) and grabbing the object without looking. If your child does this, it's because you always hold the object in the same place relative to him. All you have to do is throw your child a curveball by placing the drink (or toy or whatever) in a different spot than you normally do. Your child will reach for it, miss, and then have to look. If your child has excellent peripheral vision, you'll have to hold the object a little bit behind him for this to work.

Now that we know your child will look at everything you give to him, hold these objects up to your eyes as you deliver them to him. Your child will spy the object, and oftentimes will look at you as well. You've just created some eye contact! So hold that action figure (or drink or carrot or whatever) right on the bridge of your nose between your eyes, two inches in front of your face. You're helping your child immensely just by doing this.

Get Excited! (Celebration)

Remember earlier in the book when we talked about how you react? You're going to put this into practice in several areas, and eye contact is one of them. This means when your child looks at you, celebrate it. You can do this in several ways:

- Tell your child that you love it when she looks in your eyes
- Let loose a fun and big exclamation (like "wow!" or "yes!" or "awesome!")
- Smile big as a nonverbal way to celebrate the eye contact

These are just some suggestions. Feel free to say or do whatever comes to mind. Your sincerity is powerful and your child can sense it. If you are excited about your child looking at you, express it in whatever way you feel it. If you are not excited about your child looking at you, don't fake the celebration. Instead, get in touch with how important it is for your child to look at you (and other people), and get excited!

There are some children who look enough that if you celebrated all the times they looked at you, it would be overkill. Parents generally know when they're overdoing it. In this case, instead of celebrating every look, wait a bit and mention to your child that he was looking really beautifully for the past few minutes.

Also, if your child is talking, don't interrupt him to tell him that his eye contact was great. In this case, wait until your child is done speaking and then tell him how much you appreciate the look.

You Have to Ask for It

When your child wants something from you, ask her to look at you before you give it to her. Say it clearly and directly: "If you want the truck, look in my eyes." It's okay if she doesn't look, and you'll still give her the object in the end, but you have to ask for it. Most important, you have to show her that *when she looks at you, she gets things faster than when she doesn't look at you.*

When your child wants something to eat, take a small amount of whatever it is she's eating (like one chip instead of the bag) and ask her to look at you before you give it to her. Stay standing so she can't reach the food. After she tries (whether she succeeds or not, you want to reward the effort), give her the food. When she eats it, go back and get another small amount of food. Request her to look again. This is much better than just giving her the whole bag of potato chips, because you get several requests in instead of just one.

Working on the Docks

Sometimes people ask, "How does it help children to look at you when they weren't actively choosing to do so?" The answer is that it's similar to working on the docks. When you work on the docks, you're generally doing it for one reason: money. But you can't help but work your arm muscles as you lift all sorts of boxes and things. So even though you aren't trying to build up your arm muscles, it happens anyway. You're working the muscles so they get stronger. You might get a better workout than the guys who go to the gym three times a week and eat PowerBars and have cool duffel bags and everything.

Similarly, your child is building up the "muscle" to improve eye contact even though she doesn't mean to be working on it. Just by doing it more than normal she gets better at it, just as the dock worker gets stronger after a month on the job.

To Review:

- Eye contact is vital to your child's development.
- It's the heart of interaction.
- The more they look, the more they learn.
- Mostly, we delude ourselves about the level of our child's eye contact.
- Position for it.

- Hold objects up to your eyes.
- Celebrate looking.
- Ask for it.
- Feel appreciation when your child looks at you.

#3

Join with the Stims

*How to create a deeper relationship
with your child*

The Master of Spin

When my friend Raun was eighteen months old, he was different than other toddlers his age. He spun plates on the floor over and over. He didn't ever look at anyone. He didn't speak at all. His parents took him to a doctor and were told Raun was "uneducable." He was given an IQ test and scored just under 40. (The average American's IQ is 105; an IQ of 70 or lower is considered mentally retarded.)

He could spin cardboard boxes on one corner in such a way that his father, no matter how hard he tried, could not replicate it. Raun was a master of spinning.

This made sense, since that's pretty much all he did each day. He'd spin a plate, twiddle his fingers as it slowly came to a stop, and then spin it again. Raun was diagnosed autistic, and his parents were told that nothing could be done to help him. Luckily, they didn't believe that. Instead, they created a way of joining in with his "stimming" (not copying him; it's different) that enabled him to ultimately emerge from his autism. Doing the stim with him was one of the most important factors in his development. This is one of the groundbreaking principles of the Son-Rise Program.

Some People Call Them Stims...

Perhaps the most easily identifiable characteristic of people with autism is their willingness and/or need to do self-stimulating, repetitive behaviors. Don't get thrown off by that last sentence. That's just a fancy way of saying that your child does behaviors to enter his own world. You already knew that. These "stims," as they are popularly called, are how your child removes himself from the outside world.

Some common stims:
- Repeatedly rolling a ball down a slide
- Lining up objects (such as toy cars) on the floor
- Looking at the same books/magazines/pictures
- Watching the same DVDs, or the same scene in a particular DVD
- Constantly being on the computer or watching someone else on it
- Water play

There are countless variations of stims. Some children stare at the walls, while others draw feverishly.

How Do I Know If It's a Stim?

The thing that separates a stim from a normal behavior is that a stim is done *exclusively*. Your child does the stim on her own, without any interaction with another person. One of the great clues that something is a stim is the lack of eye contact. Notice how much your child is (or isn't) looking at other people as she does the activity.

One time, I was working with a family who was having a hard time spotting their child's stim. We had videotaped both the mother and the father working with their little boy, Billy. Billy lined up stuffed animals on a table. His father spoke to him and Billy did not respond. When we watched the videotape of the session, his father didn't understand why I thought, in that example, Billy was stimming. I walked up to the television screen and, using my palms, covered the father's image. Now we could only see Billy placing stuffed animals on the table in a focused manner.

"Look," I said. "See how when we look at Billy here, we would have no idea that someone else was in the room? He's giving no indication that you exist." I then moved my hands and this time covered up Billy.

"Now, if we look at you, you are giving off many indications that someone else is in the room. You are looking at someone, making gestures and facial expressions, talking. If I couldn't see Billy, I would think you had an invisible friend."

The father was giving off all sorts of interactive cues, which were easy to pick up on. Billy was giving off no interactive cues. Billy was exclusive. His father was interactive.

Watch your child carefully. Notice all the times he doesn't seem responsive when he is doing an activity—even if the activity is something that is considered socially appropriate. Children can stim on a book, on a TV show, or while surfing the Internet. The question is not "Is this age appropriate?" The question is "If I were to interrupt my son as he was doing his activity, would he stop what he was doing? Would he give me focused attention?"

We All Do It—But There's a Difference

Sometimes parents say to me that they have stims as well. There is often a concerned look on their face as they confess. *Is this okay? Am I a little bit autistic too?*

We all do exclusive activities. Reading a book (to yourself) is an exclusive activity. But there is a major difference when you do an exclusive activity and when your child does one: if the house were on fire, and you were reading a book (or watching a movie, or just zoning out), someone could run into the room and say, "We've got to get out of here now," and you would put down the book and leave the house immediately. You would join the interactive world at will because you were never that far away. But with the vast majority of autistic children, telling them that the house is on fire will not tear them away from their stim. Most would go on stimming as if you hadn't said anything at all.

While you can rejoin the interactive world anytime you want and stay for as long as you want, your child either can't do that or frequently chooses not to. Either way, it's a clear and noticeable difference.

Other Types of Stims

Stims are not limited to activities with objects. As I mentioned earlier, a child could stare at the wall exclusively and it would be a stim. Other varieties of stims are verbal or physical. Some children with autism will repeat favorite lines from DVDs they've seen, or sometimes entire scenes from movies. Other children might sing the same song, or part of a song, over and over. Some kids just like to say people's names or ask questions that follow an exact routine.

Some kids hop from one side of the room to the other, and then back again. Others climb the slide, go down the slide, climb the slide, go down the slide, over and over. Still others will spin themselves well past the point of dizziness.

Whatever the type of stim your child is doing, the things you always want to be on the lookout for are:

- Is my child's behavior repetitious in some way?
- Does my child make eye contact as he does this behavior?
- Does my child seem to be in his own world as he does the behavior?

Important: It is possible that your child can speak to you while doing a stim. Oftentimes we assume anytime a child speaks to us that he must be interacting with us. But it's like when you are talking on the telephone to your mother and reading or responding to your email at the same time. You can make enough responses to the telephone conversation to sound like you are paying attention, but really, you're reading your email and mostly not paying attention to your mom. When she stops talking, you fill in with a few words: "interesting," "sounds good," or even just "hmmm." But even though your mother thinks you are listening, you aren't.

So even though your child is responding to you verbally, this is not necessarily an indication that he is in the interactive world. Eye contact is a much stronger and more reliable indicator.

Why Does My Child Stim?

I've worked one-on-one with approximately eight hundred children with autism, and all but one of them had stims. Over the years, it has become clear to me that children have different reasons for stimming. These are the most common reasons, based on my experiences:

It satisfies some physical need.

A lot of children are hyposensitive or hypersensitive to things. These sensitivities may revolve around particular sounds, types of physical feelings, or even vision. A child who has hyposensitivity in his hands might tap them repeatedly or even slam them against a wall to try to feel something. A child with hypersensitivity to sounds might cover his ears and sing songs to try to repel other sounds that he cannot control.

It's a vacation from an overstimulating world.

There was a commercial, back in the day, for Calgon soap. It showed a stay-at-home mother being overwhelmed with messes, phones ringing, dogs barking, food burning on the stove, and her kids yelling, all at the same time. Completely at a loss for what to do, she yells, "Calgon, take me away!" Suddenly there is soothing music, and the mother is luxuriously lathering soap on her arm as she takes a relaxing bath. Calgon somehow transported her away from all the craziness, and she was happy, at ease, calm.

Stims work in a similar manner for many children. There is so much going on in the world to take in: dogs barking, people talking to each other, the way the wind moves through the trees, the sounds of cars going along on the road, different smells, and so on. A child with autism will often find it too much to deal with. But the child has the ability to simply escape from the interactive world that we inhabit and suddenly be in his own exclusive world. This way, the child can regulate the amount of stimulation he receives.

It's a way of having control over things in an unpredictable world.

Children with autism have very little control over most things in their lives. They are moved from one place to another, often without knowing why. Think about when you take your child to the doctor's office, or when you leave the park to go home. It's almost always on your schedule. Parents come up to their children and stick tissues against their faces without warning (to wipe off noses), or put a pullover sweater on them seemingly from nowhere. (Remember what it was like as a kid, when someone would put a pullover on you? It was dark, and uncomfortable against your face. Now imagine what it's like if it's a surprise when it happens.)

All these things that your child has no say in happen in his life. Imagine if it were you. Suddenly someone has put you in a chair. Why? You don't know. (It was lunchtime.) Or someone takes away your toy. Why? You don't know. (You were in a toy store and it was time to go.) Or out of nowhere you are lifted up and swung around; it makes you feel a little sick and dizzy. You don't know if it will stop. Why is this happening? You don't know. (Your father got home from work and came up from behind you and swung you as a way to say hello.)

These things happen all the time. So what's an autistic child to do about it? Well, you could always go into a stim. Pretend for a second you are a child with autism. Let's say your favorite stim is dropping a blue block onto a green block. Think about how you always know when the blue block is going to drop. You know how high it will be when it drops. Nothing happens with the blue block and the green block without you deciding that it happens.

In a world where you, as the child with autism, have almost no control of anything, you have all the control here.

It feels good.
A nine-year-old boy named Jackson had autism. He flapped his hands repeatedly. His parents worked with him (using the techniques outlined in this book) and by the time he was eleven, he had developed to the point where he could have conversations. He also stopped flapping his hands. His mother had always wanted to know why Jackson flapped his hands so much. Since he could now speak, she asked him:

> "Jackson, why did you used to flap
> your hands so much?"

> Jackson looked right at her and said,
> "It just felt so good, Mommy."

Though there are other possibilities, these are the most common reasons children stim. With each of these possibilities, the child has a very good reason for stimming. It is often assumed that stims need to be stamped out. But why would you want to make your child stop doing something that serves him? More to the point, it's almost impossible to get your child to stop doing something that he sees as beneficial to himself.

A Different Approach

Since your child is doing these stims for a reason, you're going to have to take a different approach than what you might expect. Going to war on the stims is only going to make your child pull away even deeper into his world.

1. Look at this chart and put a check mark next to the activity you would have the least interest in doing/learning about:

Activity Check Mark

Fishing	
Knitting a sweater	
Learning how to speak Hungarian	
Shooting a 3-point shot (in basketball)	
Long division	

Whichever activity you checked, we're going to call that "The Task." So, whenever I say The Task, you just substitute the name of that activity in its place.

2. Think of your favorite movie.

3. Imagine you are sitting in a room, watching it for the *first time*. Imagine it's about 65 percent of the way through the film. This means you are completely into it, and have already spent at least an hour watching it.

4. Imagine that a man who you have never seen before walks into the room. He sees you are watching the movie. He is an expert at The Task. For some reason, it's very important for him to teach you all about The Task as soon as he can. You don't know why he wants to teach you something that you have so little interest in learning. And, let's not forget, you are in the middle of watching this great movie.

What can the man do to get you to learn The Task?

Option 1: He could try interfering with your watching the movie.

There are all sorts of interfering behaviors he might try. Think about how you would feel and how you would react if he did any of these as you were in the middle of watching your favorite movie for the first time:

- He might stand next to you and start talking about The Task, and just keep on talking and talking about it.
- He might stand in front of the television screen and say something like, "It's really time for you to learn about The Task now."
- He might turn off the television and just begin teaching you The Task.

While there are probably endless variations on these interfering behaviors, you probably have a pretty good idea about how you'd feel and react if someone was interfering with an activity you thought was important and were completely engrossed in. Having taught parents for many years, most describe feeling annoyed with interfering behaviors like those mentioned above.

Now, if the man only needed to teach you about The Task for ten minutes one time, he might not care what you thought about him. But what if he had to teach you about things every day for the next year? Suddenly, what you think about him matters. Because if you don't want to listen to what he says, it's going to be very difficult for him to teach you anything at all. Your long-term educational relation-ship is at stake here, and the man completely blows it by trying to interfere with you when you are engrossed in an activity you care deeply about.

This way of approaching you isn't going to work if he wants you to learn things from him. (Imagine if the next day you saw him walking down the street toward your home. You'd probably lock all the doors!)

Let's move on to Option 2.

Option 2: He could leave and wait until you were finished watching the movie.

With this option, the man would see that you are in the middle of watching a movie and decide to come back when the movie's finished. Then, once it is done, he'll try to teach you all about The Task.

This is certainly more effective than all the inter-fering behaviors the man did in Option 1. You don't resent the guy. He has done nothing to sabotage your educational relationship. He has also done nothing to build your relationship, but at least he has some kind of a chance to teach you something.

We can conclude that this option is more effective than Option 1, but not terribly effective either.

Option 3: He could join the party.

Imagine the man walking in, seeing that you are in the middle of the movie, and instead of trying to interrupt or just leaving, he sits down and watches the rest of the film with you. What if he really got into the movie? He might laugh at the funny parts (if there were any), but not an overbearing laugh, not one to get you to notice him—just because he thought some of it was funny. He would really be as engrossed in the movie as you are. Imagine that.

Then, imagine, once the movie ended, how you would feel about this man. All you know about him is that he was clearly engrossed in the same movie you were into. You have something in common.

Did you know that all relationships are based on some kind of commonality? Every friend you have shares some common passion with you. So this man has begun a relationship with you, just by sitting near you and allowing himself to get fully involved in your favorite film.

This commonality gives him the best chance for you to be open to learning about The Task. And if you don't want to learn about that, well…tomorrow you're more likely to be open to learning about something else from him.

His joining in with you helps improve both your long-term educational relationship as well as the short-term learning opportunity. If you are deeply engrossed in something, it's really hard to teach you anything. But by joining in, he's giving himself a chance for success now and later. Doing either of the other two options either diminishes his chances to be an effective teacher (Option 1) or is simply neutral (Option 2).

Applying This to the Real World

The movie = your child's stim

The man = you

The Task = all the stuff you want your child to learn

This means that if your child is stimming, then interfering with the stim is only going to drive him further into the stim—and further away from you. This would mean that Option 3 is the most effective approach when your child does one of his stims.

You'll want to join in with your child when he's doing one of his stims. That's right, if he's flapping his hands, then you would want to flap your hands too. If he's lining up toy cars on the floor, get on the floor, get your own toy cars, and start lining them up next to him.

Remember, you have to do these behaviors with genuine interest, as opposed to going through the motions. That means if there is any part of you that thinks there is something bad about your child doing stims, you are going to want to think about how and why you feel the way you do. The more comfortable you can feel when your child stims, the more effective you will be.

More Than Just Educational

Joining goes beyond just helping your child to want to learn from you. Autism is a disorder that primarily impacts a child's ability to interact with other people. By joining in with your child, you are encouraging her to feel closer to you, to want to interact more deeply with you. So by joining, you are helping treat the autism at its deepest levels.

Sounds Interesting, but Does It Actually Work?

I have used this technique with approximately eight hundred children with autism, and it is an extremely effective technique *over the long run.* Sometimes children respond to joining right away, but mostly, they are involved in their stim. This is something you will likely have to do a lot of. The good news is that in nearly every case I have seen, when parents really do this, their child's eye contact increases and the stimming decreases.

Remember my friend Raun (the master plate spinner)? His family (Barry and Samahria Kaufman) brought him into a room and started spinning plates with him. They did this all day, every day. Ten weeks later, his eye contact changed noticeably. Within six months, he was talking, looking, and allowing people to touch him. Three and half years later, he emerged completely from his autism and was fully in the interactive world. Raun graduated from an Ivy League university with a degree in biomedical ethics, and has since had numerous friends, girlfriends, and jobs. He is, in every way, completely normal. There are no vestiges of autism. He is currently the CEO of the Autism Treatment Center of America, a multimillion-dollar nonprofit organization. His story has been profiled in books, in newspaper articles, in *People* magazine, by Oprah Winfrey, and in a TV movie of the week.

Families all over the world have joined in with their children's stims and have seen changes in their children. Interestingly enough, most autism treatments involve interfering with the child's stim rather than joining in. All I can say is this: if that worked, you wouldn't be reading this book.

Betsy

Back in 1994, a family came to ATCA with their eight-year-old girl, Betsy. She had autism. She didn't speak. She didn't really do anything, actually, except for her stim: she had tied a small piece of rope to a plastic ring, and tied a plastic bowling pin around the other end of the rope. She stood there, all day, with her right arm fully extended, holding the plastic ring. The bowling pin dangled twelve inches below. She would pull up with her wrist, and the bowling pin would jerk up and then bounce along in the air.

That's all Betsy did—just lightly pulled the ring up so she could watch this plastic bowling pin do a sort of dance. She did this for many hours per day, every day.

I would take my turn working with her, usually for a two-hour session. In those two hours, I did almost nothing but join her by creating my own ring–rope–bowling pin toy and lightly pulling up my pin in time with hers. I did this literally for hours, with almost no breaks. I really focused on the way the bowling pin jumped around. I found it fascinating.

Betsy gave me and the rest of the staff very little eye contact and no real indication that she was ever aware of anyone else.

Near the end of her family's training, I walked into their apartment after the work for that day had ended. I needed to get a form signed by the father for an administrative reason. The family was in the kitchen. I walked in to speak to the father. Betsy sat at the dinner table. She looked right at me when I walked in. This was a big deal, and I stopped in place to appreciate what was happening.

She just looked at me!

I was just about to celebrate her for looking at me, but before I had the chance, Betsy jumped out of her chair, came over to me, and took my hand. I was flabbergasted.

She's touching me!

Betsy squeezed my hand and led me out of the kitchen. I followed, excited, wondering where she was taking me. She brought me into the playroom. She let go of my hand and went to get some objects on the floor. She handed me the ring–rope–bowling pin toy I used when I worked with her. She was holding her own ring–rope–bowling pin toy. She looked at me again, and then began bouncing her toy in the air, as she always had. I happily bounced along with her.

Up to this point, Betsy did not acknowledge people. For her to look at me, touch me, and invite me to play with her, even if it was on her terms, represented a stunning breakthrough. It was proof to me that the work we were doing with her was getting through. She had gone from wanting to play entirely on her own to wanting me there with her. That was the first step in a journey that would hopefully lead to her valuing being with other people even more than her stim.

A Few Odds and Ends about Joining

There may be some times where it is socially inappropriate or physically difficult to join. Some children spin for forty-five minutes, but I don't know any adult who can do that without vomiting. Just do your best. You can do a half spin every time your child turns so when he sees you, it looks like you're spinning.

Some children won't let you have any of the toy cars that they are stimming with. And every time you get your own toy car to join in with, he takes it away from you. In this case, get a toy that is somewhat similar to a car (in size or shape or color) and join with that.

If your child takes whatever object you're joining with, you can join with a pretend object. Just act like you are holding an invisible stuffed animal (or whatever it is your child is stimming with) and go to town.

If you really let yourself get into the stim, you may find that your child is stimming for a particular reason: the way a shadow falls on the floor; a particular sound that is made when she bangs two blocks together; the way a ball feels against his cheek. If you think you have isolated the reason for the stim, you can sometimes just replicate the part your child really likes (you might start banging other objects together that sound similar to the blocks, for instance).

If it seems like your joining isn't working, try moving back a bit. Some kids need a bit more space. You can also exaggerate the stims. With Betsy, there was a point when I tied a small trampoline to a balance beam and yanked on the beam. I joined her stim, but with much larger objects.

Edmond

There was a little boy named Edmond who came to ATCA from Texas. All Edmond did all day, it seemed, was run around in a diaper, holding a stick in his right hand. He made almost no eye contact and didn't speak. He spent approximately 98 percent of his time running around the room. The staff joined him for eight hours a day for five straight days, running around the room holding our own sticks. He showed almost no progress during the week-long program. His eye contact slightly increased. He was certainly stimming as much as ever. His family went home and worked with him for eight hours a day, seven days a week. They recruited people in the community to work with him in his playroom. They pretty much joined him all the time.

Eight months passed with the team joining him constantly. Then, over a period of a few weeks, Edmond really started to change. Suddenly he was focused and interactive. He looked much more and began to speak. Edmond stimmed for only 2 percent of the day, instead of 98 percent. He learned to count, to read, and to interact with people. And all his family did to get him to be more interactive was join him. It did take eight months. But that's a blink of an eye in Edmond's life. His family has no regrets about how they spent those eight months.

To Review:

- A stim is something your child does to remove herself from the interactive world.
- Your child has a good reason for doing the stim.
- Interfering with your child's stim will only drive him further into his own world (over the long run).
- The best way to help your child as he's stimming is to join in and do the stim alongside him.
- You have to genuinely get yourself interested in the stim to have the full impact.

- You will help your child to be more interested in what you have to teach, but more important, you'll help your child increase his interest in being with people.
- Joining doesn't work instantaneously. It can be a slow road. But it's the only road.

4

Respond Differently to Crying

No more tears.

The British Are Coming

In 1996, the British Broadcasting Corporation (BBC) sent a producer and a cameraman to film one family's experience at ATCA. They would use the footage to make a one-hour documentary, which would be shown during prime time in England, on BBC1. This was a huge deal at the center, as millions of people would watch the staff work with this child and learn about the treatment via the documentary. Of course, we had no editorial control, so all we could do was put our best foot forward and hope it looked good on camera. We viewed this as an extraordinary opportunity to expand the scope of the families we worked with and bring the work to Europe.

A lot was riding on what happened with this particular child and how he progressed during his two-week intensive program. We were concerned that even if he made significant progress, it would not be obvious to the layperson at home watching TV, but we felt we had to try and hope for the best.

His name was Stanley, he was five, and he had pretty much never left his parents' sides. Typically, the intensive program begins at nine on Monday morning with the parents leaving the child in the playroom with a facilitator. The playroom door is locked. Some kids have no issue with this at all and happily play with the facilitator. Some kids try to follow their parents and then give up and play with the facilitator. Some kids whine a bit and then move on to playing. Some kids cry. And some, well…some scream.

At 9:01 a.m. Monday morning, with the BBC cameras rolling, we found out exactly what kind of child Stanley was.

"He's a screamer," I said to the staff, who were eagerly awaiting a report from the playroom. Members of the staff smiled. We were *elated* that he was a screamer. This was not because we wanted Stanley to be unhappy, but because we knew that, although the TV audience might not be able to notice changes in eye contact or attention span, everyone can tell when a screaming child doesn't scream anymore. And we were confident that he would change during the two weeks.

Why He Cries: The Two Possibilities

When a child cries without having injured himself, there are only two possible reasons. Either your child is:

1. Genuinely unhappy, and crying is an expression of that unhappiness.
2. Faking it.

That's it.

Since faking it happens much more often than genuine expressions of unhappiness, we'll begin with that.

Faking It

The first thing to acknowledge is that sometimes when your child is crying or whining or making that unhappy face, she is actually feeling fine and is just doing it as a strategy to get things from you.

Huh? What? Isn't that a little sophisticated? Not at all. Every child's job is to figure out what moves their parents. All of these kids are smart enough to understand that you act differently when they are crying (or whimpering, or whatever it is they do that gets you to give them what they want).

I had a father recently explain to me that when he refuses to give his daughter a cookie, she cries. He waits a while, and then gives her the cookie.

Why does he give her the cookie? Because "she really wants it." Or because "I don't want her to be sad." I understand why parents say this, but you have to look at it from your child's perspective:

I want the cookie. I ask for it. That doesn't work. I cry. I get the cookie. Thus, crying works as a tactic to get me the cookie. Sweet! Whenever I want something that I'm not getting, I'll just cry.

It's really very basic. You have taught your child that crying works better than any other way to get something she wants. She now cries as a tactic to get what she wants. Do you see how it works?

So It Works on Me. Who Cares?

You should care for a few reasons. First, you are inadvertently teaching your child to cry more than he otherwise would, and that just doesn't make any sense. Second, *crying often will replace speech.* Why learn words when you can just cry for something? Your child already knows how to cry. Third, there are much better ways to operate in the world than crying as a way to get what you want. When was the last time you saw a drain get unplugged because someone cried? Fourth, you absolutely hate it when your child cries. You feel awful when your child cries. You want your child to cry less. So of course you should care if what you are doing is (inadvertently) encouraging your child to cry more.

Actual Emotional Distress

Certainly there are times where your child may be upset and crying from a place of unhappiness rather than faking it. The first thing for you to acknowledge is that you probably don't know which is which.

What you probably do is assume unhappiness in your child when the situation is one that would make *you* unhappy. But remember, your child is different than you. Your child is autistic, and thus has a whole different way of taking the world in. Even though you might be unhappy when you don't get what you want, your child may be feeling fine and dandy and is just doing what works to get what he wants.

I am reminded of a little boy who was crying in the room on the first morning of his intensive. He was sitting at the door, crying, "Mommy, Mommy!" and banging his head against the door. I sat down about fifteen feet away from him and began imitating him: making crying sounds, saying "Mommy, Mommy," and banging my head against another door.

The boy completely stopped what he was doing and just stared at me. Then he started laughing. I said, "Am I doing this right?" He nodded yes. He smiled at me again, then went back to crying and banging. *Nice talking to ya, I gotta get back to work now.* I imitated him again, and again he stopped and laughed. After a while, he saw that this behavior was ineffective (which was new for him—until then it had always worked like a charm) and stopped entirely. Then he calmly and sweetly played with me and the staff for the rest of the week.

What Happens When Your Child Cries

In this chart, write up the last four times your child was doing a crying behavior.

In "Instance," write the details around the incident.

In "What he wanted," write the thing he seemed to be crying to get. If there wasn't anything that he seemed to want, write "nothing."

In "How I felt," write what emotion you were feeling when your child was crying.

In "Get it right away," write if he got the object within two minutes of the crying.

In "Get it at all," write if he got the object of his desire within thirty minutes (FYI, if you promise to take him to McDonald's and you do, it counts as him getting it, even if it takes longer than thirty minutes).

Instance	What he wanted	How I felt	Get it right away?	Get it at all?
Breakfast this morning	Waffles instead of oatmeal	Really bad	Yes	n/a

Look at your chart. Notice how often your child gets what he wants when he cries. Is it 25 percent of the time? Fifty percent? One hundred percent? Don't be alarmed—most parents give their child what they want after a crying behavior at least 50 percent of the time. We have been trained as parents to do this. When our kids are infants, the primary way they communicate is by crying their heads off. *I'm hungry! I have a wet diaper! This hurts! I'm tired!* It's all communicated the same way. You learn to do the thing that soothes your child. The thing is, we often mistake this communication for unhappiness—even in babies. Just like with autistic children, they may be unhappy some of the time. But most of the time, it's simply a standard communication technique. Your kids may still be using crying as a standard communication technique. Or they may be using it tactically to get what they want because they know it works better.

The other thing to look at is the "How I felt" column. You might be expending a lot of energy feeling bad when your child is just doing what he knows to do to get what he wants.

How to Deal with It: When They Are Acting Unhappy

Okay, so there are the two possibilities (emotional distress and faking it) that are present whenever your child is doing any type of crying behavior. With each possibility, there are two aspects to dealing with the crying: what you do externally and what you do internally.

Let's start with the notion that this time when your son is crying he's faking it, and that he's acting unhappy because it's a successful tactic to get what he wants. If this is the case, then it would be foolish for you to get all bent out of shape when he's crying. Think about it: he is feeling calm and peaceful inside and is putting on a performance, and you are upset about the fact that (you think) he is unhappy! If he's faking it, you wouldn't want to buy into pretend unhappiness and get unhappy yourself. You'd just be expending emotional energy. If you know your child is feeling okay, it should be easy for you to feel that way too.

Let's say your daughter wants a bowl of ice cream and you've told her that she can't have a third bowl. She starts crying, and you recognize that she is probably acting unhappy as a way to get more ice cream. You remember that she's probably feeling okay underneath her tears, and so you feel okay too. Nice! Now, here's what you do:

Start moving more slowly than you normally would. I don't mean slow-motion slowly, but you want to move slower than normal to illustrate to your child that this tactic of acting unhappy is having the opposite of the intended effect. When children cry, most parents begin to move much faster than normal, scampering around the room, trying to offer the correct thing to get the child to stop crying. The child sees that you've suddenly become The Flash, and mentally notes that once again, there is power in acting unhappy.

To counteract this, you want to show that not only does the crying not make you move faster, but in fact, it makes you move more slowly than before. If your child has lots of language challenges, then you deal with this by acting confused. You're not sure what it is your child wants. You're trying to be helpful, but you don't really know what to do. So, you go around the room, offering lots of things to your child, but not the thing she wants. This way, you present yourself as helpful and on her side. You just aren't sure what to do to help. If you consistently slow down and don't give your child what she wants when she cries, she will begin to adopt other communicative tactics. You can also say things like, "I want to help, but I don't understand what you want. Try telling me."

If your child is more verbal and has clearly requested something from you, then you still want to move slowly, but you also have to tell your child that crying isn't going to get her another bowl of ice cream. You can, in a calm and easy way, explain how she's not going to get any more ice cream regardless of whether she cries or not. You can also offer other possibilities (foods she can have). As your child learns that the ice cream isn't coming even if she cries, the crying will diminish.

Important: Because your children have such incredible radar for how you are feeling, if you do all this but feel terrible while you do it, you still are paying them off, to some extent, for crying. You have been affected and they can see it. It's still a powerful thing they can do. If this is the case, the behavior will take much longer to diminish.

How to Deal with It: When They Are Genuinely Unhappy

If your child is genuinely unhappy, you would want to address the emotional implications of this with your child. That doesn't mean to tell your children what they are feeling by saying "You're unhappy," "You're sad," etc., because you don't know for sure how they are feeling and you don't want to mislabel emotions. Instead, you need to help them learn to feel comfortable in the situation where they are uncomfortable. The best way to do this is for you to feel calm and peaceful, as a way to model to your children that it's possible to feel comfortable in the very situation that they are struggling with.

Children look to adults (and their parents in particular) for cues on how to respond to situations. A great example is when a one-year-old falls on the ground and all the adults around him stop to see if he's okay. Most of the time, the child looks up to the adults before he reacts to the fall. I have seen so many children fall, look up to their parents (who have a look of deep concern or worry on their faces, or might even be saying, "Are you okay?" in frantic voices), and then start crying as a result. I'm sure you've seen this play out many times. I have also seen a child fall, look up, and the parent smiles and says, "You're okay, come here!" with a playful voice, and then the child reacts by getting up and rejoining the play with a smile. Children often take their cues from us.

The same is true of your autistic child. If your child is uncomfortable, then you can help her by showing her that you feel okay in the situation. By doing this, you teach your child that she can feel comfortable in this situation, too.

You have to remember: you have a huge impact on your child.

Don't worry about how you have been up until this point. It's okay if you've been doing the opposite of everything I'm advising you to do. Most parents are doing all the most ineffective things to deal with their child's crying. Then they learn to do these techniques and their child usually responds quickly, with crying behaviors decreasing and language increasing. If your child learns that crying doesn't work so well as a way to communicate, he will search for other, more effective ways. This opens the door to increase language development with your child.

What Happened with Stanley

The BBC filmed the family for two weeks. Stanley's parents would enter the playroom twice a day to work with him for fifteen minutes each, and then leave to receive training. Stanley cried for his mother for the first two and a half days, especially when she left the room and it was just him and a staff member. On Wednesday, I walked into the room to work with him. He and his mother were playing with a car. I walked up and took her place. She left quietly. Stanley didn't cry or even seem to care that she left the room. That was it. Stanley didn't cry for the final week and a half of their program.

Stanley also developed in other notable ways: his speech increased, his eye contact went way up, he began dressing himself, and he even taught himself to use a microwave oven! The documentary aired in England in September of 1997 and was the highest-rated show in its time slot. Europe became very interested in our work and, since then, ATCA has run seminars with hundreds of parents every year in European countries.

To Review:

- There are only two reasons why your child is crying if he hasn't been injured: he's genuinely unhappy or he's faking it.
- You can't tell the difference between actual unhappiness and faking it, even though you probably think you can.

- If your child is genuinely unhappy, it's important that you feel as peaceful as possible.
- If your child is faking it, it's also important that you feel peaceful.
- Move more slowly when your child is crying, so she learns that crying is less effective than other forms of communication.
- You can do this.

#5

Give Your Child as Much Control as Possible

Hands off, Buster

The Girl Who Wouldn't Leave the Bathroom

One time a girl named Heather and her family came to ATCA. She was nine years old and had an interesting way of shutting out the world. She went into the bathroom (which was attached to the playroom), closed the door, and refused to open it.

Heather did not speak. We could look into the bathroom through a two-way mirror, so we knew she was safe. I was the second person to come into the playroom on that first morning, and there she was, parked in the bathroom.

I tried to talk to her through the door.

The only response was a loud scream.

"All right, Heather, it's up to you. But I want you to know that anytime you want to come out here, there's food and things to drink, and toys." More screams from the bathroom.

I said more things like that to her, and was met with the same screaming response. Eventually, in an attempt to lure her into the playroom, I began playing with toys in a fairly noisy (and hopefully interesting) way just outside the door.

This failed miserably.

Eventually, I gave up and decided to place my attention elsewhere. I got a storybook from the shelf, sat in the opposite corner of the room, and began reading the book out loud. I read it in a normal-volume voice. I wanted her to hear me, but not necessarily make out the words. Most important, I wanted her to think I wasn't reading to her.

As I reached the fourth page, I could hear the bathroom door open slightly. Behind the crack, Heather was watching me. I said, "Come on over and sit with me; we can read the book."

She screamed and slammed the door. This was going to require a little more subtlety. I went back to reading the book out loud, in the same tone of voice as before. After a few pages, I again heard the bathroom door open. This time, I kept on reading the book, acting as if I did not realize she was there. I read for four more pages, by which time the bathroom door was completely open and Heather was staring unabashedly at me.

I looked up and softly said, "Do you want to come see the pictures?" With a huge smile, Heather skipped over to me and plopped down on my lap. We read the book together, and Heather didn't close herself in the bathroom for the rest of the week.

What happened here? Why did I let her stay in the bathroom? Why, once she came out of the bathroom, did she stay out for the rest of the week?

In a word, it was all about control.

What Is Physical Manipulation?

Physical manipulation is when someone forcibly moves another's body against his will. Some common examples of this in life:

- Police restraining a prisoner.
- A mentally ill patient, who is dangerous to himself and others, being put in a straitjacket.
- Holding someone down who wants to jump off a building to commit suicide.
- Pinning someone's arms behind his back to break up a fight.
- Wiping your child's nose with a tissue without warning.

There are many ways most parents physically manipulate their children. The "Wipe Without Warning" is a favorite of many. Your child has a runny nose. He won't let you get close to his face with the tissue, so you just wipe his face anyway. A popular adaptation of this old favorite is to come from behind him so he doesn't see it coming.

What's the big deal? Well, tell your spouse to take a tissue and come from behind you and wipe your nose. But tell your spouse to do it sometime over the next two days, so you honestly don't know when it's coming. See how you like it.

Of course, the "Wipe Without Warning" is just one of many common physical manipulations parents do to their kids. Here are some others:

- Holding down a child's legs so he stays on the toilet.
- Pulling the shirt over his head without warning.
- Pulling a child away from a toy or activity she was interested in.
- Forcing a spoonful of some food in his mouth that he clearly doesn't want.
- Pushing the dining room chair so tightly against the table that she can't easily get up from dinner.
- Hitting your child.

Remember, autism is all about an interaction void. We want to give your child as many reasons as possible to interact with us, as opposed to giving him more reasons to avoid interaction. When we physically manipulate, we give him more reasons to shut us out.

It can be easy to forget that we are much bigger than our children. When you pull that shirt over your child's head against his will, it is similar to an eleven-foot giant forcing you in the same way. Imagine being the smallest person in the land of the giants, and they move you around all the time without warning, explanation, or any obvious reason. This is similar to some children's experiences. I remember when I was taught this Son-Rise Program concept. I was amazed at how little I had thought about moving a child without his permission.

Make a list, right now, of the ways you physically manipulate your child.

Now take a look at the list. Don't even think about feeling bad or guilty about this. You did what you knew to do. It's what everyone always does. As a parent, you are always doing the best you can with the information you have available to you. Now you know more than you did before. Don't worry, nothing is damaged. You just have to change how you physically interact with your child to foster a more trusting relationship.

What to Do Instead

So you're at least partially convinced that moving against your child's will is not a great idea. Cool. Here's another way to wipe your child's runny nose:

1. Take a tissue and hold it three feet or so away from your child, in his line of sight.
2. Move slowly.
3. Tell him what you are going to do. For example, you could say, "I'm going to wipe your nose now."
4. Move slowly toward his face.
5. If he pulls back, stop moving forward. Wait a moment, then slowly continue toward his face with the tissue.
6. If he continues to pull away, stop. Explain again what you are doing and see if he moves closer to you. If he does, continue. If he doesn't, put the tissue down.
7. If he pushes your hand away, let him. Don't fight it.
8. Wait a few minutes and try again.

This may take a while, because your child is exercising some control that he isn't used to having. He may want to test it out some.

It's better to let the nose run than to move against your child's wishes when you don't have to. The amount you gain in future trust and rapport more than compensates for the mucus going down your child's face.

An Example of Rapport in Action

One time I worked with a little boy named Todd. He always fought like crazy whenever it was time to get a haircut. His parents described it as a nightmare, which always ended in his screaming and kicking, and very little hair being cut. I decided to try to build trust around haircutting. I brought a pair of scissors into the playroom and placed them on the shelf. Todd and I played with toy cars for a while. At some point, I got the scissors and brought them over to Todd. He pushed them away.

I immediately put them back on the shelf and said, "Oh, okay, no scissors." A while later I brought them down again. Again he pushed them away. Back on the shelf they went.

After a while, he began playing with a stuffed bear. I told Todd that the bear needed a haircut. We set up a stool in front of a big mirror and sat the bear down. Todd then ran to the corner of the room as I brought down the scissors. He watched intently as I gave the bear a quick trim.

"Now it's your turn," I said. "Come on over here." Todd walked carefully to the stool and sat down. He could see everything that was happening because the mirror was right there. I very slowly brought the scissors down and cut one strand of his hair. He allowed this, but then stood up and walked to the other side of the room. I waited. He smiled, and sat back down on the stool. He let me cut another strand of his hair.

I had shown Todd that he could trust me, that nothing was going to happen without his permission. He was peacefully getting haircuts within weeks.

This is what you want to engender in your child. When there is something hard, scary, or unfamiliar that you ask your child to do (like looking at people more often, speaking more often, eating different foods, etc.), the more trust that you have built up, the more likely it is your child will try these things.

Giving control is all about building trust and a relationship with your child.

Safety First: Sometimes You Have to Physically Manipulate

Sometimes physical manipulation is unavoidable. There are times where your child's safety is endangered. Then you do whatever you have to do to protect your child. Relationship goes out the window until everyone is safe.

One time a family was at the intensive program, and I had just taught the parents all about giving their child control. Somehow, their four-year-old autistic son had gotten out of the playroom and ran into the parking lot. The boy was sitting right in the middle of the lot, throwing stones onto the ground. His father, armed with fresh knowledge about giving his child control, spent about forty-five seconds trying to coax his son back into the apartment.

I knew that cars often entered the parking lot at high speeds, and thought that this boy's safety was at risk. I asked the father if he minded if I stepped in. He seemed very happy to let me take over.

I walked up to the boy and told him I was going to pick him up if he didn't walk back to the apartment right away. He continued throwing rocks at the ground, and made no movement toward the apartment.

I stepped closer and picked him up. He resisted, shaking himself back and forth violently. I began walking back to the apartment with him struggling in my arms.

I calmly told him: "I'm doing this to help you. I want you to be safe. Inside you'll be safer."

Suddenly, he completely relaxed in my arms and allowed me to carry him the rest of the way with no resistance.

Why did he stop resisting? Did he understand me? I don't know (he wasn't speaking yet). He may have. He may have picked up on my calmness throughout the experience and calmed down as a result. He may have just gotten tired of fighting. Regardless, the point is that *I was not going to let him stay in an unsafe situation.* I would worry about rebuilding trust and relationship with him later.

Notice how I still spoke to him, giving him a chance to go back into the apartment of his own accord and understand why this was happening to him. When you have to physically manipulate your child, use both your words and your tone to explain to him what is happening, why it is happening, and that it's okay that it is happening. You can model feeling comfortable in this situation.

Most parents feel fear or anger when they are forcing their child out of an unsafe environment. Try feeling peaceful, even as you take clear and strong action. This can help your child move more easily through the experience.

To Review:

- Physical manipulation is when you physically move against your child, either because she has shown you that she doesn't want to be moved, or when done without warning.
- Avoid physical manipulation whenever possible.
- By giving your child more control, you are building a significantly deeper and stronger relationship with your child from *her point of view.*
- Tell your child what you are going to do before you do it.
- Do things that will impact your child in front of him so he can see them coming.
- Respect your child's NO signs: pulling away, pushing your hand or the object away, saying "no," etc.
- Know that sometimes you do have to physically manipulate your child, mainly for safety reasons.
- If you do have to physically manipulate your child, don't be wimpy about it. Be clear and strong. Try to feel calm inside as you do it.

#6

Focus on
Your Attitude

Perhaps the most important piece

The Little Laugh

One time, near the end of my child facilitator training, a family from Portugal came to ATCA with their son Jose. There was a translator in the playroom at all times, because none of the facilitators spoke Portuguese, and Jose spoke in sentences. He was a sweet and charming young man, and we all had a great time working with him. On the third day, I was playing with him and, out of nowhere, he pulled down his pants and peed on the floor.

I laughed slightly and encouraged him to go to the bathroom to finish the job. He just stood there urinating. I got paper towels, came back, and cleaned up the mess. This kind of thing happened sometimes, so I didn't think much of it.

But about seven minutes later, Jose pulled his pants down again, and everything repeated itself: he peed on the floor, I laughed slightly, I encouraged him to go to the bathroom, he finished and pulled up his pants, I cleaned up the mess. I thought it was strange that it happened again so quickly, and decided to observe him closely.

Sure enough, about ten minutes later he pulled down his pants and peed again. I laughed, I tried unsuccessfully to get him to the toilet, he finished, I cleaned up.

I tried to get him to play in the bathroom with me, so the toilet would be close by if he peed again. He refused.

It happened again, ten minutes later. And again. And again.

Six times in ninety minutes! *That* was completely unusual. And he hadn't done this behavior with anyone else. I didn't understand why he had done this with only me. I thought long and hard about it that evening.

And then I figured it out: I laughed. Just slightly, yes, but every time he peed, I uttered a little laugh. It was a reaction. Jose had picked up on my little laugh, noted it as a reaction to his peeing, and then kept on doing it.

I laughed like that because I wanted him to know that his peeing on the floor didn't bother me. Of course, if it didn't bother me, why would I need to show him that? I knew based on all my training that giving no reaction at all was *by far* the most effective way to respond to his peeing. I had demonstrated the ability to not react to these types of behaviors for the past several months. But for some reason, I was giving a reaction to the peeing. Why?

As I thought about it, I knew the answer: the translator. I wanted the translator to know I was not bothered by the peeing. I cared what the translator thought about me. I could remember a feeling of emotional discomfort when Jose peed on the floor, because of my concern about how the translator viewed me.

This is one of the two main reasons why how you feel matters: you are unable to act clearly and do all the things you know to do when you are uncomfortable. I found myself giving a reaction even though I was accomplished at not reacting to these types of behaviors. This is something I see all the time in my work with families. Parents don't celebrate when their child says a new word because they are uncomfortable about something else and in that moment, they just can't remember to celebrate. When you are uncomfortable, it's almost impossible to keep it all in your head.

This is why we don't perform as well when we are nervous. The discomfort takes up space in our mind and we are unable to fire on all cylinders.

The Other Way It Works

The first way attitude impacts your time with your child is by making you less able to access the knowledge in your brain. But there is a second, and even more important, way how what you feel impacts your work with your child: *it has an effect on him*.

Remember, autism is an interaction disorder. We want to make ourselves and the people around us as attractive as possible to your child. Think about what your child is drawn to. If you are sad, or angry, or frustrated, or bored, you are significantly less attractive as someone to interact with.

I have described people who facilitate children with autism as commercials for interacting with the rest of the world. If you are angry, sad, bored, etc., your child will assume other people are likely to be this way as well. If you are happy, at ease, feeling good, etc., your child will be more drawn to interact with you and other people in general.

Think about it from your child's point of view: it's already difficult to interact with people. Why would he give all this effort to interact with someone who was unhappy?

If you feel bad as you work with your child, you will be less effective because 1) you won't be able to focus the way you would if you were comfortable, and 2) your child is less interested in interacting with someone who is unhappy.

You Can't Fake It

Children with autism have an extraordinary ability to sense people's emotions. It may be because most of these kids are not as focused on speech as the rest of us are, and so they are more attuned to nonverbal cues. Many speech therapists say 80 percent of communications received by children below the age of three is nonverbal. This means your child is paying attention to all of these things:
   • Your tone of voice
   • Your facial expressions
   • How you move your hands
   • How you are breathing
   • The speed at which you talk
   • The speed at which you move
   • The words you say
   • Probably some other stuff, too

You just can't fake being happy because there are so many different signals you are giving off in any moment, and your child is paying attention to them.

So I am not advocating you act happy when you are not feeling that way. It is far more important for you to feel how you actually feel and not attempt to cover it up. *If you are not feeling good, then it's something to examine so you can learn to feel differently when you are with your child.*

When You Feel Uncomfortable

It's time to learn more about how you tick. Here are some tools to do research on yourself.

Let's start by being clear about what the phrase "how you feel" means. It means how you feel *emotionally*. It is not what you are thinking. Some examples of how someone might feel are:

Happy	Sad
Joyful	Scared
Comfortable	Resentful
Angry	Guilty

There are certainly many more words that describe feelings. What you want to avoid are phrases that describe a situation or your assessment of the situation, rather than your emotions (for example, the response to "How did you feel?" wouldn't be, "I felt that I was doing a good job and that he responded well." It would be, "I felt good," "I felt angry," or some other word that describes your emotions).

In this chart, write about five times you felt uncomfortable around your child and what was happening just before you felt this way. Don't worry, no one else is going to see this.

Times I Felt Uncomfortable with My Child

How I felt	What happened just before
Angry	My son pushed down another child at the park and everyone looked at me.

Look at what you wrote and see if there are any patterns. Do you feel uncomfortable consistently when your child seems unhappy? Or is it when she won't do what you want? Is it when she's stimming?

Think about why you feel bad when these things happen. Usually, when people think about the reason for their discomfort, they come up with a quick answer that is often wrong or, at least, a surface answer. We're used to justifying our discomfort: "I was angry because no one should yell at me like that!" But that is a weak answer. It doesn't explain why you felt the way you did, though it does sound good to friends when you tell them the story. And it allows you to never have to go any deeper with the question.

Because we are talking about changing how you feel, you have to understand why you felt the way you did. Let's look at some events where people often feel uncomfortable, and some possible surface answers and honest answers, so you can get a feel for this.

Event: My boss yelled at me.

Question: Why did I feel uncomfortable?

Some possible surface answers:
- "No one should talk to me that way."
- "It was inappropriate for him to yell at me."
- "He's a jerk."

Notice how all of these answers do not explain why you felt the way you did. You could have any of the three thoughts above and still could feel peaceful.

Some possible honest answers:
- "When someone yells at me I think I have done something wrong."
- "I want to tell him off and getting angry gives me the strength to do so."

Notice that with these answers, either the boss's yelling is interpreted to mean something or anger is used as a motivator.

"When someone yells at me I think I have done something wrong." I am interpreting the yelling as meaning I did something wrong. Note: this is different than "I did something ineffectively." If you think you do something ineffectively, then you just learn to do it differently. When you think you've done something wrong, then you are judging it as bad, and *as soon as you judge something as bad, you feel bad.*

"I want to tell him off and getting angry gives me the strength to do so." This time, I am using anger to motivate myself. I want to tell him off, but I don't have the courage. Then I get angry and I do it.

Most of the time you feel unhappy it is because you have interpreted something that happened as bad for you or because you are trying to motivate yourself to do something you otherwise wouldn't do. For more on this, read *Happiness is a Choice* by Barry Neil Kaufman.

A Quick Example

Lee was a nine-year-old boy with autism. One of his major challenges was that he often banged his head against walls. I was working with his mother, Joy, and we had this exchange:

"How do you feel about him banging his head?"

"Terrible," said Joy.

"Why do you feel terrible?" I asked.

"Because that's not right for a boy to do."

This was a great example of a surface answer. Often, we hear an answer like this and we stop asking because we think it would be disrespectful to dig deeper.

"What do you mean?" I asked.

"If I can't stop him from banging his head, I must be a bad mother."

"Why do you believe you would be a bad mother if you can't stop Lee from banging his head?"

Joy looked confused. "No one ever asked me that before."

"Just go with it," I said. Because the Son-Rise Program is the only treatment to focus on how parents feel as they work with their child, the questions can sound unusual at first.

"Because he could hurt himself. A good mother wouldn't let her son hurt himself...of course, I'm not letting him do it. He does it any chance he gets."

"So why would you be a bad mother?"

"Maybe I wouldn't be...all I can do is try, right?"

The honest answer below the surface for Joy was that she thought she would be a bad mother if he kept doing what he was doing. It's easy to brush over that, but by examining it she gave herself a chance to feel differently about it. As a result, she became more comfortable with his head banging. Lee stopped banging his head after a while because it didn't provoke the same reaction as it used to.

Look back at the chart you made earlier in this chapter. The circumstances that led to your feeling uncomfortable are only the first part of unhappiness. The second, and much more significant part, is the way you interpret these events.

This is because *what you believe about the events around you leads directly to how you feel about them.*

Your Deeper Reasons

Take the information you wrote in the chart, and this time add in the honest reason why you felt the way you did.

The Honest Reason Chart

How I felt	The circumstances	The honest reason
Angry	My son pushed down another child at the park and everyone looked at me.	I thought they would think I was a bad parent.

Look carefully at the reasons you wrote. Do you see any patterns? Make sure that the reasons are about your interpretation of the event or that you're using the discomfort to motivate yourself to action.

As you look over your reasons, ask yourself one of two questions:

1. Why did I believe that the event meant what I thought it meant? (If your reasons are about how you interpreted the event.)

2. Why do I need to feel discomfort to motivate myself? (If your reasons were about motivating yourself.)

Note: Certainly there can be other reasons why you feel bad or unhappy about something. When you answer these questions, be open to the following ideas:

1. You don't have to interpret the event as "bad."
2. You can motivate yourself to do something without having to feel bad first.

If you don't judge something as bad, and you trust that you will motivate yourself with desire alone, you'll start to feel a lot better.

In the end, all of this helps your child. The more you feel comfortable in these previously challenging situations, the more you can impact how your child behaves in these circumstances.

To Review:

- How you feel emotionally greatly impacts your child's experience and makes a difference.
- Pretending to feel good is ineffective.
- People get unhappy about things because they judge them as bad, or to motivate themselves to take action.
- Delving into your deeper, honest reasons for your unhappiness is a key to feeling differently.

#7

Work One-on-One in a Non-Distracting Room

Where the work gets done

The Three Environmental Factors

Everyone learns better in environments suited to effective learning. Put another way, how well do you think you'd learn Swahili if it was being taught in the middle of the New York Stock Exchange, with people yelling and pushing everywhere?

There are three factors to consider when looking for an optimum educational environment for your child:

1. Level of distraction.
2. Level of control.
3. The emotional attitude of the other people around your child.

Level of distraction

Your child is surrounded by colors, noises, and movements. Many autistic children cannot process large amounts of stimulation. They become overwhelmed. Think about how your child does at birthday parties or the mall. If he gets overwhelmed, then you know he is overstimulated.

Even the children who enjoy all this input are often caught up in all the things going on around them. Have you ever tried to teach your child something while he was watching a DVD? Nearly impossible, right? That's what environments that have a lot of kids, colors, or sounds can be like. You have your child's attention sporadically at best. Your child will learn fastest in a setting that has few, if any, distractions.

Level of control
We talked about control in terms of physical manipulation in a previous chapter. Now we are going to go a step further. It's important to give your child as much control as possible. This means that you need to create a situation where you don't have to refuse your child very often. By doing this, you make the world around your child significantly more attractive, so he'll be more motivated.

Obviously you shouldn't give your child everything he wants. But wouldn't it be nice for both of you if you could say yes more often? Most of the time, your child is not allowed to do the things he wants. He can't touch the things in the room that look interesting to him because he might break them. He can't stick his hand in the toilet because he might put it in his mouth.

The more you give your child the things he wants, the more he will want to interact with you. Most environments are set up so you have to say no to your child:

Outdoors: He may run into the street, or just run away, so you may have to physically restrain him.

In a friend's home: He may break your friend's iPod, or want to take off his clothes, or pee on the floor.

A grocery store: He might want to eat foods he's allergic to.

Your kitchen: Watch out for the knives, etc.

Your other child's bedroom: He wants to take all the best toys for himself, and now your other child is upset.

A classroom: Kids have to sit most of the time and focus on a teacher-directed activity; he might want to do other things.

These are just a few examples of the world your child lives in. It is a world of "no." The more you have to say no, the less your child is going to want to interact with you. There are times that refusing your child cannot be avoided wherever you are, but your job is to minimize this.

The Attitude of Other People around Your Child

Remember how important your emotions are? Your child will generally interact more with someone who feels good and interact less with someone who feels bad. When you are with your child, you are more than just yourself: you are a representative for the human race.

Other people also represent the human race to your child. When your child comes into contact with people who are judging him or the things he's doing, that matters. It makes being with people less attractive to him.

This is true even if people are not judging your child. If they are just uncomfortable around him, he will still be less inclined to interact with them. As a result, it's important to try to keep your child out of situations where others are likely to be uncomfortable for any reason. Unfortunately, that is most public places. Almost everywhere you go will have people, and it's likely that some of them will feel uncomfortable around your child. Choose environments that will shield your child from these attitudes. For now, we want your child to think everyone in the world is a pretty happy person. Later on, we'll let him know that it's not always like that.

Remember, you and everyone else your child encounters is an advertisement for interaction.

At the beginning of this chapter, I asked you how you'd do learning Swahili at the New York Stock Exchange. Let's go a step further now: how do you think your child would do learning at the NYSE? It posts failing grades on all three key environmental factors: it's hugely distracting; there is certainly no control; and it's fair to say most stock traders aren't having a peaceful, happy experience while they are working the Exchange floor.

Whenever you are not sure about how effective an environment will be for your child, fill out this chart:

Place	Distractions	Control	Attitude	Total
The circus	1	2	3	6

Write the name of the place you are considering taking your child. Then, under each column, rate each factor between 1–5. One is very poor; 5 is excellent. I have included an example of the circus. I rated it a 1 for distractions (with all those things to look at and noises), a 2 for control (your child has to stay in his seat and isn't free to move around very much), and a 3 for attitude (people are generally happy to be at the circus, but you have no idea who will be there). The total is a 6.

Scoring is easy. Anything below a 12 is a poor place for your child to learn. Low scores, especially around control and attitude, may encourage your child to go even deeper into his own world.

Is School a Good Place for Your Child?

Most parents have their children in schools. Is this a powerful place for your child to learn the skills he needs? Let's take a closer look. Most schools place kids with autism in one of two situations: a room full of other autistic children or a regular classroom filled with kids their age.

Let's examine both of these settings in terms of their effectiveness for a child with autism.

Classroom full of autistic children

In this case, usually there are four or five teachers for a twelve-student class. This number can be higher or lower, but it's close enough. Usually the children in the classroom make messes, need to go to the bathroom, stim, hit themselves or each other, etc. The teachers basically run around putting out one fire after another, with very little time ever put toward helping the children learn anything. The only peer models are other autistic kids, and I have had parents tell me how their child learned new stims from copying other kids in the classroom.

Snack time in a class like this takes a very long time. Nothing is routine or easy. The teachers, though very dedicated, often have little training in dealing with children with autism. So, in the times when there are no fires to put out, there are 0.3 teachers per child available to teach the kids. This is a very low number because the kids are usually at different skill levels. Your child may get forty-five minutes of actual teaching each day.

This is not to denigrate the school systems and the job they do. They have limited resources and do an excellent job considering the circumstances. Most likely, however, you can do a better job.

Putting your child in a classroom with other autistic children is basically killing time for your child. While some children do progress in school systems, the vast majority of parents are dissatisfied with the education their school provides.

Classroom full of typically developing children
By typically developing, I mean a regular classroom

filled with non-autistic "normal" children. The practice of putting children with autism in a regular classroom is called inclusion.

One of the things that is problematic in an all-autistic classroom is not an issue in this setting: your child has peer role models who are interacting in typical ways. However, that is pretty much the only positive factor in this setting. In a regular classroom, there are usually one or two teachers, and the autistic child gets an aide who sits with him and helps him to do whatever the activities are.

Okay, let's list the problems with a regular classroom:

1. The curriculum is not designed to help your child with autistic challenges. Instead of working on language or eye contact or attention span—the things your child really needs help with—he is doing complimentary skills that have little relative value, like math.

2. The other children may model behaviors that you wouldn't want your child doing (like breaking objects, yelling, hitting, and swearing). In most cases, all of these behaviors are given big reactions by both the other children and the teachers, which make it more likely that your child will do them.

3. There is a lot of noise and color in the room, providing distractions for your child.

4. That noise and color in the room is over-whelming for some children with autism.
5. The child has no control when he is in the class-room. He cannot stand when he wants to, go where he wants to, talk when he wants to. The activity is chosen by someone else, which makes it uninteresting to your child (in most cases).

The truth is that inclusion is a nice thing for the non-autistic kids in the classroom because they learn to look after someone and be more caring. But for the child with autism, it is usually a waste of time.

Don't Make Academics a Primary Focus

Many people get caught up in teaching subjects that are typically taught to kids. This mainly consists of reading, writing, math, spelling, grammar, etc. There's a reason why they teach these subjects in school: these are the skills children need to succeed in life. The thing you need to realize is, the kids who learn this in school *already have interaction skills down pat.* They don't need to be taught to look at people or how to speak. They are being taught skills that will help them manage at a higher level in life and get jobs.

Your child does not have interaction down. If he did, he wouldn't have been diagnosed autistic. If you are working on teaching your child academics instead of interaction skills, *you are helping your autistic child to have skills that he won't be able to apply.* This doesn't mean to say autistic children cannot learn math or reading or writing—quite the opposite. Many of them are tremendous readers, and some do math at a very high level. But if you are teaching your autistic daughter spelling, what are you building toward? Is it that you want her to grow up to be a woman who spells extremely well but is still autistic? Believe it or not, the world is full of this type of people already.

Very often, parents (and school systems) teach academics to children with autism because that's what we generally teach all children, and people don't know how to teach interaction.

This doesn't mean that you won't need to teach your child to read or write or anything else. But for now, *don't make academics a primary focus of your child's education.* This is a big mistake!

What You *Can* Do

Start regularly working with your child one-on-one in your home. I normally recommend that parents pull their child out of school and work with him in their home full-time, but that's not always an option for a lot of parents. That's okay. Start working with your child for an hour every day after school.

Rearrange a room in your home that will double as your child's workroom. Oftentimes the child's bedroom is best, but if you have a spare room, that works even better.

Make sure this room is non-distracting. That means taking the posters off the walls and confirming it is in a quiet part of your home. Pick up the toys so the floor is clean. Remove any electronics. These are primary distractions for most kids. You can't compete with things that are naturally more interesting than most interaction. You want to set up this room so people are the most interesting things in it. Take out any electronic toys as well. Anything that beeps or has lights generally is fascinating to children and again, you can't compete.

Also, make sure this room gives your child maximum control. Take anything out of the room that your child can't have or play with. Leave any toys your child stims with in the room. Exception: if your child stims on the television or any electronic device, take it out. These things are too compelling.

If you do this, you will have created an environment that is safe and non-distracting, gives your child control, and shields your child from the negative attitudes of other people. This room would score very high on the environment chart! Interestingly, this idea started when Barry and Samahria Kaufman worked with their son Raun in their bathroom. It worked so well, they have since used special rooms with each child in the Son-Rise Program.

Go in the room, close the door, and play with your child. Get out some toys or games that she likes and try to interact with her. If she stims, join her. If she looks at you, celebrate her. If she doesn't look like she's doing anything, start up a game and see if she wants to play. If she doesn't, try another one. If she goes back to stim, you go back to joining. Try to say yes to as many of your child's requests as possible. Have food and drink available so there's no need to leave the room. Have a potty in the room so she can go right there. If she uses a toilet normally, take her to the bathroom just before you go into the room.

All you are trying to do is create a situation where your child is learning about how great it is to be around people. By doing this in a distraction-free environment where she has control, you are giving her the best chance to learn about being with people.

Things That Come Up When You Do This

There are some reactions children may have to being in a locked room. Here are the two things that come up the most.

More stimming

When you put your child in this environment, her stimming may increase. This is because you have removed the distractions of the outside world, which, when your child is distracted by them, can be a form of stimming unto themselves. Think about how much you interact when there is a television on in the room. Most people will admit that their eyes are constantly going back to the TV screen, even if they're interested in the conversation. We are less interactive when there are distractions. This applies to your child as well. If you remove the distractions, your child has to do something to block out the world instead of just getting caught up in all of the noises, colors, etc. Trust me when I say that putting your child in a non-distracting room doesn't make her stim more. It just makes her stimming much more obvious to you.

He wants to leave the room

This is a very common issue. Up until now, your child could go wherever he wanted in your home.

Suddenly, you want him to stay in the same place for an hour. It wouldn't be surprising or unusual if he wanted to leave the room.

If this happens, there is an easy solution that a lot of parents have a hard time with. Lock the two of you into the playroom for the hour.

Lock the door? But what about all those paragraphs about giving him control? How does he have control then? Well, in the case of the door, he doesn't. But he has control over everything else that happens in the room. You won't be able to find any other room in your home (or anywhere else) where this is true. You may have to lock the door, but by doing this, you are locking out all the times you would otherwise have to say no to your child. You are also locking out all the distractions. Here's what usually happens when parents lock the door to the room.

The child:

1. Whines or cries for a while;
2. Tries to open the door;
3. Tries to get the adult to open the door;
4. Whines and cries for a bit longer;
5. Tries to get the door open some more; and then
6. Gives up and begins playing with the adult.

It's important to remember that this is a very common reaction and all you have to do is show him that the door isn't going to open, no matter how much he protests. Once your child learns the way it works (that the room allows him to do things he can't do anywhere else), the locked door ceases to be an issue.

Other issues

There are other possible issues that you may encounter when doing this. In the end, the approach is pretty much the same no matter what the issue is: you want to follow through on the amount of time you had decided to be in the playroom and trust that this is the best place for your child to learn about being with people.

What You Have to Remember

Your child does not have the same kind of expectations about the world that you do. It's not necessarily strange to a child to suddenly be in a room with an adult for an hour (or more). Although many children with autism have particular routines, they usually adapt quickly when given the chance. It's up to you, as the parent, to give your child a legitimate chance to adapt to this new situation.

I was working with a family recently when the father, Herman, asked me about the room.

"How could anyone stand to be in a room like that?" asked Herman.

"Well, it's all how you frame it," I explained. "How would you like to be in a place where you can do pretty much anything you want, and the person who is there with you cheers you on, does any activity or game you want, leaves you alone whenever you want, and is totally enjoying everything you do all the time?"

"That sounds pretty good," said Herman.

And that's how you want to look at this room. It's an incredible place and your child may not have figured that out yet. It's your job as the parent to show your child how great it is.

By the way, Herman's son *loved* the room from the get-go.

To Review:

- There are three main factors that determine the quality of an educational environment: the level of distraction, the level of control your child has, and the emotional state of the other people in the environment.
- A school setting is not an ideal place for an autistic child.

- Academics are not the most important thing for your child to learn right now. Leave them until after he's mastered the skills of eye contact, attention span, speech, etc.
- Working with your child one-on-one in your home gives your child a great chance to learn at a faster rate.

#8

Be Dynamic with Your Child

*How to make yourself instantly
more interesting*

The Secret Ingredient

Joey wouldn't use the toilet. It was one of his biggest challenges. He had other issues—his eye contact and speech both needed work—but his parents were most concerned with his seeming love of diapers.

I observed his mother request that Joey try the toilet, to sit on it at least. Joey happily ignored her, and instead played with the stuffed rabbit that he always carried around with him.

"C'mon, Joey," she said. "Just try it. Do it for Mommy."

Joey wasn't biting.

Later, in our training session, his mother expressed frustration and hopelessness about Joey ever using the toilet. I was going to offer her some suggestions, but before I had a chance, we heard shouting coming from the playroom.

We rushed in to see what was happening. Joey was sitting in the corner, holding his rabbit. Sally, an ATCA facilitator, was jumping up and down and shouting, "C'mon Joey! C'mon, the toilet is waiting for you!"

We smiled because Sally looked funny. But something interesting happened. Joey stood up, rabbit still in hand, and walked over to the toilet.

"He never even gets that close to the toilet," said Joey's mom. "How did she get him to do that?"

"That's the power of enthusiasm," I said.

Enthusiasm

In all the years I've been doing this, with all the children I've seen, one of the most consistent things I've observed is that nearly every child responds to enthusiasm.

Kids love cartoon characters. Wile E. Coyote is a favorite because when he falls off a cliff, first his feet go, then his body...then, finally, after an expression of concern, his head. It's funny. It's a much bigger way of having the character fall off the cliff then to just have him go down the way something normally might. Think about cartoons: the explosions are bigger. On the old *Batman* TV show when Batman or Robin punched a bad guy, the screen would suddenly be filled with a word, like "THWACK!" or "BAM!" Kids loved that show. The attention kids give to these dynamic moments is what you will take advantage of by being enthusiastic.

Many parents think of their children as a bit frail, that someone who has a lot of energy and enthusiasm could overwhelm their child. This can be true if the environment itself is very distracting or if the child is stimming at the time; otherwise, it is almost always false.

By working with your child in a non-distracting environment and having enthusiasm, you stand out tremendously.

The application of this Son-Rise Program concept makes the staff at ATCA noticeably different than most other professionals who work in the autism field.

But I'm Not Naturally Like That

If you are someone who claims to not be a very enthusiastic person, you are fortunate because you can actually *learn* to be more enthusiastic.

The first thing you have to do is to feel some enthusiasm about working with your child. If you are not excited about that, then this chapter will only teach you how to fake it. Your child will be able to see right through that. If you are having problems feeling enthusiastic about spending time with your child, fill out the chart below and refer to the "Focus on Your Attitude" chapter.

This chart is designed to help you build your feeling of enthusiasm. Write the skill you want your child to learn in the first column, and then the benefit to your child or your family in the second column. I've included an example for you.

Things I Want to Help My Child Learn

What I want my child to learn	What this will result in
Eye contact	A deeper connection with her, feeling closer, something that will help her learn faster.

Now that you've filled this out, read it over. Does it get you pumped up? If not, fill it out again, really paying attention to the "What this will result in" column. If you are clear about the benefits of working with your child, it will be easier to feel excited.

Many people tell me that they feel some enthusiasm inside, but don't know how to express it. Here's how to do that.

The Three Tools of Enthusiasm

There are three things you can do to make yourself express your enthusiasm. They are:

1. Vary your tone of voice.
2. Vary your facial expressions.
3. Vary how you move your body.

The point is: you want to have "dynamic variation," which just means you change your presentation often enough so you are continually interesting.

Good public speakers do this all the time. They are regularly moving around, changing their intonation and pitch, offering different facial expressions. Often, the most compelling stories are when the speaker reads in the different voices of the characters. It's much more interesting to hear a Sherlock Holmes tale when every time Holmes speaks you can hear his English accent.

One of the most fascinating parts of varying yourself is that you will be more interesting to your child, yes...but *the time will be more interesting to you.* It's more fun to vary your voice, your face, and your body.

Varying your voice

It's interesting to a child when you sometimes speak in a voice that is different than your normal one. People have no problem doing this with infants when they think no one is watching. I've seen a stuffy English accountant, thinking he was alone, do all sorts of baby talk.

You *do* have it within yourself to make funny voices. Let's do some exercises, shall we?

Get yourself and your spouse (or a friend) alone in a room. If you don't have anyone to do this with, don't worry about it. Go into a room by yourself.

Here's the sentence we're going to be using:

"The robots have cleaned up the dog pound."

- Say this sentence using your normal voice. (No problem, right?)
- Okay, now say that same sentence, only now say it much louder. Pretend you are in a big room and you have to make sure someone at the other end of the room can hear you.

- Now, say the sentence in a whisper. (You're just getting warmed up here.) And by the way, really do this. I don't care if you "know you could" do it—actually say the words right now.
- Say the sentence the way Darth Vader would say it. (If you don't know who Darth Vader is, I don't think I can help you. Think extremely low-pitched.)
- Say the sentence in your normal voice, but very quickly.
- Say it extremely slowly, like you are in slow motion.

And that is how you vary your voice. You can do many other voices, but this exercise is designed to give you an opportunity to experiment with your vocal ranges. High, low, fast, slow, loud, quiet. When you vary your voice, you become more interesting.

This doesn't mean that you should never use your normal voice. Absolutely use it. But sometimes, add some pitch to it. Add some volume to it. Speak a little slower or faster. You now have yourself an enthusiastic-sounding voice.

Varying your face

Everything you learned about your voice is also true with your face: you have it in you to do this and people do it all the time when they think no one is watching. So we're going to skip right to the exercises.

Get a partner and go into a room where you are alone. If you can't get anyone to do this with you, get yourself in front of a mirror. Remember that all the instructions mean for you to move your face *without your hands* or anything else besides your facial muscles. After each instruction, bring your face back to a natural, relaxed state.

Are you ready? Good. Here we go:

Either look at your partner as you both do the instruction, or watch yourself in the mirror. Relax your face.

- Look at your partner's face (or your own in the mirror). This is the "normal face."
- Smile a big, wide smile. Don't worry, it's supposed to look unnatural.
- Make the biggest frown you can.
- Scrunch your face up. Try to get your chin, forehead, and cheeks as close to your nose as possible.
- Now make your face as big as it can go. Open your mouth wide, spread your cheeks, lift your eyebrows.

- Pretend that there are strings attached to your cheeks and they are pulling, one left, one right.
- Now pretend that there is a string attached to your forehead and another attached to your chin. The one on the forehead is pulling up, the one on the chin is pulling down.
- Try to make your face look like a blowfish.
- Pretend you are a fish that has been hooked, and you are being pulled up to the surface. What does your face look like now?
- Look surprised.
- Look happy.
- Look thoughtful.

Not so bad, right? If you are finding it hard, just remember that I do this exercise live with parents *all the time*. Just try it again until you have a handle on it.

It's not that you always need to have a crazy facial expression, but you want to be able to pull one out when needed. When you are celebrating your child looking at you or saying a word, having an interesting facial expression makes the celebration stronger.

Varying your body
The same rules apply for this exercise as the facial one: you either want another person to do this with

or a mirror so you can see yourself. In this case, you want a mirror big enough to see your whole body.

At the end of each instruction, bring your body back to its natural stance.

- Stand in your natural stance.
- Open your arms as wide as possible, as if you were going to give a hug to the fattest man in the world.
- Open your arms wide, and step one foot far out in front of the other. Hold this position for a second.
- Walk around the room like you are the Energizer Bunny. This means you are very stiff except for your right hand, which you are banging the bass drum with.
- Walk around the room quickly, but with extremely small steps.
- Walk around the room slowly, but with very large steps.
- Get as low as you can to the floor and walk around.

This is all you need to do—just to have some dynamic ways of moving around, speaking, and making your face do interesting things.

Don't Overdo It

You could take what you learn in these exercises and decide that you have to be this extreme person all the time. But don't do that. Instead, you want to become a hyper-real version yourself. This means, when you are unsure about something, you have a bit more of an exaggerated "thoughtful" look on your face. Or when you are celebrating, you want to celebrate bigger than you normally would.

It's important that you don't go too far with this and become someone your child has never seen before. Think of it this way: if you were a 5 before (on a scale of 1–10), you want to be a 7 now. Just try to bump yourself up two points. If you are already a 10, no need to go any higher.

Some Kids

There are some kids out there who do not respond well to this type of enthusiasm. If this is the case with your child, don't be overly enthusiastic. As with everything in this book, do the things that work with your child and discard anything that doesn't. However, don't be so sure your child won't like enthusiasm. Nearly all do.

Kirk

There was a family that, after we spoke about enthusiasm, the father, Kirk, really seemed to get it. He went into the playroom with his daughter and she began dropping cream cheese on the floor and sort of ice-skating on it. Kirk, who normally would have cleaned up the cream cheese right away, instead began whooping it up and skating around the room with his daughter. Twenty minutes later she was in his arms, laughing and looking at her daddy. Later, Kirk pulled me aside and said, "That was the most fun I've ever had with my daughter. And it was so easy!"

To Review:

- Enthusiasm is a powerful tool that you can use with your child.
- There are three ways to express your enthusiasm: in your facial expression, your tone of voice, and how you move your body.
- Even if you think you are naturally a quiet person, you can do this.
- Don't fake it; your child can sniff that out. Let yourself genuinely feel enthused!

#9

Get More Language

You know you've been waiting for this chapter

Matt and Janice

I was working with a little boy named Alex. He was nine years old, and his family had been to ATCA the previous year and had returned for further training.

Alex talked a lot—he could speak at least five hundred words—and yet there was a big problem. Nobody besides his parents could understand him. Alex would say the beginnings of words, but only sometimes say the middle, and never the end. He might look at me, with a big smile on his face, and say, "Look over at that man," except it would come out: "Lou oh ah tha mah." Alex's parents, Matt and Janice, understood him. It's like when you see a movie with heavy English accents—at first you don't know what the actors are saying, and then you suddenly understand them. Matt and Janice had adapted their hearing to Alex's way of speech, so much so that I believe Alex thought he was speaking clearly.

After working with Alex, I pulled Matt and Janice aside and explained that a huge vocabulary wasn't useful for Alex if they were the only ones who could understand it. It was unlikely that most people would be willing to take the time to try to understand Alex.

"We've been working on building his vocabulary," Matt said proudly.

"Yes, I see that," I said. "But no one besides the two of you can understand him. I really think you have to focus on his pronunciation skills."

They paused and thought about this.

"We haven't ever focused on pronunciation," said Matt.

I could tell.

There's a Lot to Say

When I train groups of parents about how to help their children improve their speech, I talk for two hours without a break. Then, when the presentation is over, I am deluged by parents with more questions. There's so much to cover with speech, there's probably a book in there all by itself. Speech therapists make a career just on their expertise on this subject. There's a lot to it.

The most important principle to know is that *speech is communication.* You want to teach your child to communicate—not to know some words. The more your child wants to communicate with you, the more language your child will want to learn, and the faster this process goes.

Watch What You're Saying!

Oftentimes, parents get so caught up in wanting their child to speak that they become poor models for speech themselves. You want to model correct and useful speech to your child. Some common issues are:

- **Speaking very quickly.** A lot of times parents so want to express their enthusiasm through their speech that they end up talking so quickly that they are difficult to understand. Also, you may teach your child poor pronunciation habits.
- **Describing everything.** Many parents will offer a description of what their child is doing: "You're going down the slide. Now you're climbing up the slide. Now you are going back down the slide. You're walking over to the table." This is not what you want to do, because this is not communication. No one speaks to each other like that. Don't model this for your child.
- **Speaking very slowly and in a boring manner.** You don't want to put your child to sleep! You

want your speech to be compelling so your child will pay more attention to you and learn to speak faster. The more motivated your child is, the faster he will learn.

- **Speaking in generalities.** If your child is saying fifty words or less, avoid generic words such as "it" and "this" and "that." I can't tell you how many children learn these words and then use them to describe all objects (for example, pointing at a teddy bear and saying, "I want this"). While this has some use, if your child doesn't learn more vocabulary, it's not going to work for him in the long run. A rich vocabulary allows your child to communicate with all people, and in more sophisticated ways. That means he'll get what he wants faster. Other "vocabulary killers" are the words "more" and "again." Once a child learns those words, she can say them without needing to learn any other words. That's not going to work for her in the long term either. Don't worry if you've been doing these things. I'm going to show you how to motivate your child to learn a larger vocabulary.

Do You Hear What I Hear?

At ATCA, we sometimes did something called video feedback. This was where we would videotape a parent working with her child and then watch the tape with the family, pointing out both effective moments as well as areas the parents could alter their technique to help their children more.

I was doing a video feedback with Samantha, one child's mother, and Kerry, the child's grandmother. Samantha had been in the playroom with her son Robert. Samantha very much wanted Robert to speak. He had never spoken. We began watching the tape.

Something interesting happened about five minutes into the tape.

On the tape: *Robert was on a wooden slide, and Samantha said, "Do you want to come down?"*

"Come down," said Robert. Samantha didn't do or say anything.

This would have been a great opportunity for Samantha to celebrate Robert speaking.

I stopped the tape. I looked at Samantha and Kerry. They looked a little confused.

"Why did you stop?" asked Samantha.

"He's never spoken before, right?" I asked.

"Right."

"Why didn't you celebrate his speech?" I asked, genuinely curious. Parents usually are over the moon when they hear their child speak for the first time.

There was a very interesting pause.

"What do you mean?" asked Samantha.

I was about to go into an explanation of celebration and reactions, but there was something about the way she asked the question that led me to think she meant something else.

"What were you thinking when he spoke right there?" I asked.

"When he spoke right *where?*" Samantha looked confused. Kerry looked at me as if I were crazy.

These are the times I am thankful for videotape.

"Let me show you what I mean." I rewound the tape a little and hit the play button.

Robert was on the wooden slide, and his mom asked him if he wanted to come down.

"Come down," Robert said. I stopped the tape and smiled.

Samantha and Kerry looked at me, their faces full of confusion.

"When does he talk?" asked Kerry.

"He just said 'come down,'" I said.

"I didn't hear anything," said Samantha.

"Okay," I said. "Let's play it again."

This may seem exaggerated, but I played that video at least four more times before they heard Robert say "come down." It got to the point where I paused the tape just before he spoke and said, "Okay, listen right here."

It was like one of those Magic Eye pictures that

were popular in the nineties. You look and you look and you look some more, and you just can't see anything but a field with flowers. Then, suddenly, you see a spaceship. And it's easy to see the spaceship from then on.

That's how it was with Samantha and Kerry. They just couldn't hear Robert's words, and then, one time, finally, they heard it. They made me play the tape several more times, because they wanted to hear him speak over and over. They were hugging and laughing—they were extremely excited.

But they hadn't heard anything when he actually did speak. Or when they watched a video of it several times. Why was this?

I believe it is about expectations. They had known Robert his entire life, and they thought of him as a child who did not speak. I knew they said Robert did not speak, but I had been trained to be open to anything the children might do. So when he said "come down," it was clear to me. Even when I played it repeatedly for Samantha and Kerry, pointing out exactly where it was, it took them six times to hear it! That's the power of expectation.

You have to listen carefully: your child may be saying more than you think. If you ask a question, your child may not answer it for a few minutes. Remember what you ask your child, and expect an answer. But especially, *listen*.

Placing Your Child on the Language Spectrum

There are a few factors to consider when you try to access your child's language abilities. They are:

- Vocabulary
- Pronunciation
- Length of sentences (how many words are in your child's sentence? One, two, five, ten, etc.)
- Ability to have conversational give-and-take (having multiple comments and responses in an interaction that are connected)

  Example:

  Child: I want milk.

  Mother: We're out of milk. You can have juice or water.

  Child: I want water. When is Daddy coming back?

Fill out the following chart to get a better sense of where your child fits in on the language spectrum. Circle the box in each row that best describes your child's language ability.

Language Abilities

Vocabulary	0–5 words	6–20 words	21–50 words	51–300 words	300+ words
Pronunciation	Poor	Fair	Pretty good	Very good	Excellent
Sentence Length	1 word	2–3 words	4–6 words	7+ words	
Conversational Give and Take?	No	Yes			

Another way to think about this is that there are some kids to whom language is a primary issue, some where language is important, and some where it's a secondary issue at best.

The Three Types of Kids
Language as a primary issue
Most children who are diagnosed as autistic or on the autistic spectrum fit into this group. These kids do not speak at all, speak very little, or have poor pronunciation. They may make many sounds that are indistinguishable, or they may, like Alex from earlier in the chapter, say many words that only you and your spouse can understand. With children who have these types of challenges, language is a key

issue. You still have to prioritize interaction and eye contact with your child. This is because the more interested your child is in interacting with you, the more he will try to communicate.

Language as an important issue
Some children with autism can speak many words with fairly good pronunciation. They can verbally communicate what they want and understand the usefulness of speech. However, they may not have a large enough vocabulary or their pronunciation may still need work. These children will use speech for what they want, but not necessarily participate in a full conversation. They are most likely not asking other people questions. Language is clearly an important skill for these children to work on.

Language as a secondary issue
Some children can speak with relative ease. They have very large vocabularies, speak clearly, and can participate in some back-and-forth with others. There are still some issues: pronouns are often challenging; questions and comments made by the child may be repetitive; the child may not listen well; and conversations may be limited in scope. These children still need to work on language, but it can take a back burner to other issues, such as potty training.

Go For It

When language is a primary issue, parents are often encouraged to use communication aides. These usually include a picture board (where a child points to a photo of a toilet if she has to use the bathroom) or pictures on flash cards. Sometimes children are taught sign language.

In general, these approaches are a mistake. Your child becomes interested in only what is going to help him get what he wants, rather than learning to speak. It is significantly easier for a child with language as a primary issue to point to a picture and get what he wants. Why would the child ever try to learn language? What's his motivation? *Children learn language fastest when that is what's asked of them.* There are certainly cases where a child is helped by pictures or sign language to learn speech. In most cases, however, it's easier for both the adult and the child to rely on nonverbal communication, and thus speech development is slowed significantly.

The other thing to remember about these is if your child does not learn to speak, you can always use a picture board or sign language later. Because these can help with effective communication (though nonverbal), if you teach them to your child first, what's the point in learning to speak (from the child's point of view)?

It's okay if you've taught your child sign language or used a message board or pictures up to this point. We're going to cover how to motivate your child to speak shortly.

What to Teach Your Child to Say

Many people are clear they want to teach their children to speak but don't know which words to teach. We've already talked about the problems with words like "it," "that," "this," "more," and "again." Here are the types of things you want your child to learn:

For a child with language as a primary issue:

The main thing to work on is action words. Children will always learn the words that have the most power for them the quickest. Here are some examples of action words:

- Tickle
- Up
- Down
- Eat
- Drink
- Bounce
- Throw
- Pull
- Push

- Roll
- Squeeze
- Sing
- Swing

With each of these words, note that if your child says it, you can give a clear and strong response. For example, if your child says "throw," you can throw him a ball. If he says "eat," you can give him a banana. These words all have a payoff that you can deliver to your child. This is important because the payoff is what will motivate your child to try to learn and say the words.

Let's figure out some quality action words for your child to learn. In this first chart, list the things your child likes you to do for her. Your participation is vital here. If your child doesn't need you at all to do this activity, then it doesn't belong on this list.

Things My Child Likes Me to Do

Activities/Games

Tickle her	
Blow on her face	
Chase her around the room	
Feed her	

You now have a list of actions that we can assign words to. It's important that you pick only one word to represent the action, and that you are consistent with it. You wouldn't want to call eating "eat" on Monday, "food" on Wednesday, and "lunch" on Friday! That would only confuse your child, and then she might think she has to learn three different words for this activity. Keep it simple for her and pick one word that you are going to use for all eating activities. If she has a word she normally uses and it's correct, go with that. For example, if she already says "food," then there's no need to change the word. But if she says "buchoo" when it's time to eat, you'll want to teach her a word everyone can understand, like "eat."

It's time for you to pick some words to teach your child. Referring to the chart, write down your child's favorite activities that she needs you in order to do. Then, write a word that describes the activity. Try to keep the word short; one or two syllables are fine.

Assigning Words to My Child's Activities

Activity/Game	What you'll call it
Pulling her by her feet	Pull

Now you have a list of possible words to work on with your child!

For a child with language as an important issue:
Usually a child who has some language skills has been taught words that are not useful or powerful. A vast amount of kids in this category learn words like "please" and "thank you" and "I want." None of those have any real impact on communication. If your child says "book," and points to the bookshelf, he's communicated that he wants a book. There's no added impact by including the words "I want" at the front of the sentence.

This is in stark contrast to your child adding speech that has real power to the word "book": descriptors like colors ("green book"), sizes ("big book"), or types ("*Sesame Street* book") work best.

"Please" and "thank you" are social norms that, in most cases, are not important to your child. In fact, most non-autistic children don't care about "please" and "thank you" either. They say it to appease their mother who is standing over them—usually after they've been prompted to say it.

Sometimes parents want their autistic child to learn to say things like "please" and "thank you" so their child will seem more normal. If this is you, even just to a small degree, read this next bit carefully.

Your child is not normal. He has autism. Getting him to look a little bit more normal is just wasting energy that could be spent on learning things that will be of use to him, like eye contact or more useful words. Please understand that there's nothing wrong with not being normal. It's wonderful how unique and brave kids with autism are. So stop trying to get your child to look normal and focus instead on helping him where his biggest challenges lie.

You want to focus on descriptors (as mentioned a few paragraphs ago), clarity of speech, and increasing sentence length.

One of the easiest ways to teach descriptors is to have a few options available when your child makes a request. For example, if your child says "ball," hold up two different-colored balls and ask, "Do you want the red ball or the blue ball?"

Now your child has to say more than just "ball." You are adding to his sentence length and helping him learn words (descriptors) that will be powerful in many contexts.

If your child needs help with clarity of speech, be slower to get him what he asks for. Ask your child to say the word again, more clearly. If he says it more clearly, then get him what he wants immediately, with a big celebration. Show him that *there is power in clarity*.

Because your child has some speech skills, think about where he needs the most help: vocabulary, clarity, or sentence length.

Sentence length should only be focused on once clarity and vocabulary are not major issues. Of course, you are always going to want your child's vocabulary to increase, but here is a rule of thumb to determine if you should work on sentence length or vocabulary:

- A child with a vocabulary of 1 to 50 words will generally use one-word sentences.
- A child with a vocabulary of 51 to 100 words will generally use two- to three-word sentences.
- A child with a vocabulary of 101 to 350 words will generally use three- to five-word sentences.

Using these rules, determine where your child needs to improve. For example, if your child has a vocabulary of one hundred words and is speaking in one-word sentences, then you'll want to focus on increasing sentence length.

Remember, clarity must be strong before you try to improve sentence length.

For a child with language as a secondary issue:
For these children, language is more about helping them have conversational back-and-forth, improving pronouns, and perhaps being less rigid in how they use language.

Two key things you can do to help are modeling correct language for your child and coaching your child. Coaching works like this: your child is talking to another person (with eye contact and interaction) and you are there, listening. When you have a suggestion for your child, you lean in and whisper it to her. She can try it right then and there. This real-time practice is, for some kids, the most effective way to learn.

Remember that it is easy for people to minimize the importance of eye contact when children are this verbal. *If your child isn't looking others in the eyes very often, then eye contact remains a primary issue for you to deal with.*

Giving Good Response

A key to helping children at any level of language is giving big responses to the behaviors you want to encourage. Here's an example of being responsive to children who fit in each of the three language categories.

How the idea of being responsive would work with a child who has language as a primary issue:

Your child points to a book and says, "ruuhh."

You cheer the effort and say, "Good try. Now say book, and I'll get you the book."

Your child tries, by saying "buh."
You cheer and give your child the book.

Do you see why? Your child has made a step in the right direction. Before she was saying "ruh" for "book," and now she has the first letter. You want to reward that to help her understand that using the "b" sound at the beginning of the word will help her to get the book faster.

Note: this doesn't mean you do not give your child the book if she says "ruh" again. You might ask a third time for "book," and then give it to her regardless of what she says. But as you do it, explain that if she said "book," you would understand immediately and she would get the book faster.

This is not about keeping the things your child wants away from her. It is about showing her what works to get those things the fastest.

An example of how this might work with a child where language is an important issue:

Let's assume your child says "block" a lot, and it's not a challenge for him. But he mostly says one-word sentences and you want to help him improve this.

"Block," he says.

"Which block do you want?" you could ask. Then, you hold up a red block and a blue block and say, "Do you want the red block or the blue block?"

Your child says, "Red block." Then you cheer and give him the red block right away. And now, when he asks for a block, you can encourage the descriptor to be added to form two-word sentences.

Note that this only works if, when he says "red block," he gets the red block right away. If you cheer him but there is no payoff (in the form of getting what he asked for), then it is not powerful. The payoff is what makes learning language go the fastest, so start thinking about what kinds of things are payoffs for your child.

How this might work with a child where language is a secondary issue:

Let's assume that one of your child's challenges is that he always asks for the book in the exact same way: "I want the book."

"I want the book," he says.

"Ask me in a different way and I'll get you the book," you could say.

"I want the book."

"Try saying it differently. You could say, 'I want to read the book!'"

"I want to read the book."

"Great!" And then you quickly give your child the book.

In all three of these examples, note that the payoff is delayed until the child has attempted to do what we ask. Again, this doesn't mean that you won't give him the book, the block, or whatever if he doesn't make an attempt. Instead, you show that it takes longer if he doesn't communicate effectively.

Echo! (Echo!)

Some kids repeat whatever you say to them. Sometimes it is just the last word of your sentence; sometimes it is the entire sentence. This is called *echolalia*. Many children learn to do this because it works very well. Their parents will say sentences that, when the child repeats the last word of the sentence, work as a communication.

Here are a few examples:

Parent: "Do you want to eat dinner?"
Child: "Dinner."
Parent takes this as a yes and makes dinner.

Parent: "Do you want the green ball or the red ball?"
Child: "Red ball."
Parent gives child the red ball.

Notice a pattern here? On a practical level, this works very well for the child. If you are the child, you don't have to think much about what your mom said—you just repeat the last bit of it and it pretty much works out. You don't have to form words or sentences in your mind, and you don't have to retrieve the correct word that describes what you want. It's all taken care of for you. In fact, parents often unconsciously change their speech patterns so their echolalic child will be able to respond to them by repeating what was said.

This is a problem because we want your child to be retrieving words and forming sentences in his mind. These are vital skills to advanced communication. If your child doesn't have to develop these skills, he's not going to have conversations or be able to express himself.

There is a relatively easy way to deal with echolalia. All you have to do is make being echolalic an ineffective way to communicate, and your child will learn to stop doing it.

What I mean is, be aware of how you end your sentences. End them with words that cannot be repeated for any useful effect.

For example, instead of saying: "Do you want a tickle?"

Say this: "I'm going to tickle you in a big way!"

Or: "If you want a tickle, just tell me!"

These are just examples; you could say this in many other ways. When your child repeats the end of your sentence (like "tell me" or "way" from the previous examples) rather than a clear communication, then you get to show him that it didn't work. You do this by taking what your child said literally.

So if he says, "Tell me," you can say, "Tell you what?" This might throw off your child at first, but that's okay—it's supposed to. You want your child to see that his method of repeating what you say will no longer work. If you do this a few times, your child might get it or might repeat it more feverishly, trying to get it right. He also might cry, whine, or tantrum. If that happens, remember what you learned in the "Dealing with Crying" chapter.

Another way you can do this, if you know what your child wants, is to offer it as the first option when you give him choices, like this:

"Do you want the elephant or the bear?" (You know he wants the elephant.)

So you're showing your child the need to listen and think more. With most children, a few weeks of work is all it takes for them to move past this, and sometimes it's much faster.

It's all about this one idea: does it work for your child? If it works, he'll keep on doing it. If it doesn't, he'll adopt a new tactic.

If your child is repeating entire sentences, you still want to deal with them literally. Example:

You: "Do you want some cereal?"

Your child: "Do you want some cereal?"

You: "No, thanks, I'm not hungry right now."

You don't do this to be funny or cruel, but instead to help your child understand why he needs to think more when you speak. This also encourages him to think more about how he wants to respond. When you've got him understanding that echoing you is not effective, it will decrease.

How to Know What to Ask Your Child For

It's important to have a clear sense of what your child can and cannot say. What words are easy for her, and which ones are challenging? How many words are in an average sentence? Are there particular sounds that your child has trouble saying correctly? This knowledge will guide you when deciding exactly what to ask your child to say. The general rule is this:

You want to ask your child to do something that is *just* outside her skills.

What to ask your child to say
if he wants you to blow him a bubble

What he's actually saying	What you should be going for
No sounds	Asking for "buh," giving bubbles to any sound he makes
Indistinguishable sounds	Asking for "buh," responding to anything close to a "b" sound.
Communicative sounds (like "roo")	Asking for "buh," responding to anything close to a "b" sound.
The "B" sound at the end or middle of the sound ("roobuh")	Asking for "buh," responding to anything close to a "b" sound at the beginning of the sound.
"B"	Asking for "buh," responding to "buh."
"Buh"	Asking for "bubble," responding to anything that is two syllables and begins with "buh."
"Bub"	Asking for "bubble," responding to anything that is two syllables and begins with "bub."
"Bubble"	Asking for a 2-word sentence with descriptor word, like the number of bubbles, or big/little bubbles, or "blow bubble"
"Five bubbles"	Asking for a 3-word sentence, with 1 or 2 descriptors, like "blow five bubbles" or "five big bubbles"
"I want bubbles"	Asking for a longer sentence, like "I want mommy to blow the bubbles" or "I want mommy to blow three bubbles."

Remember: you can blow the bubbles for your child, even if he doesn't respond as much as you want. Ultimately, effort should be rewarded. You want your child to push herself because this is the learning process. So, if you are asking for "buh" and your child says "kee" three times in a row, go ahead and blow the bubbles anyway. You don't want to turn your child off from the game or from trying to speak. Once the bubbles have all popped, you can go right back to requesting "buh" again. This keeps it fun for your child, keeps her involved, and helps her to see that the closer she gets to speaking as you've requested the faster she gets her bubbles.

Once your child is saying the word "bubble," you have to remain aware of the clarity of her speech. If she is not speaking the words clearly, ask for that instead of longer sentences. Also, make sure you are getting eye contact when she is speaking to you. If you are not getting eye contact, ask for that instead of more words. Once you are getting eye contact, go back to asking for language.

This is just one example of how this can work. The important thing is to see how you are always asking your child to do something that is one step beyond what he has mastered (reminder: this works when he's motivated for you to do something for him). This way, when he is most compelled to get something, he will try the hardest.

Sometimes parents shy away from challenging their child when he's motivated. "He's having fun with me," they say. "I don't want to lose him," they say.

I understand why people think this. But it is dead wrong. This is the time when he's most likely to do his best work. You have to take advantage of that.

And yes, sometimes when you are challenging him he will walk away and begin to stim or play something else. That's okay. That's actually a good sign. If your child never walks away when you are challenging him you're not being challenging enough.

Note: Sometimes a child's skills will be different depending on unknown factors. For example, your child may say "doggie" one day, and not be able to say it the next day. That's okay—just ask for whatever is challenging to your child in that moment. If she can't say "doggie" today, then work on saying "duh." If she can say "doggie," then work on adding a second word to the sentence.

To Review:

There's a lot of information in this chapter. Here are the key concepts for you to remember:

- Be aware of how you speak to your child. You are a model for speech, and if you are modeling noncommunicative speech (meaning you describing what your child is doing instead of talking to your child) or talking so much that there's no opportunity for your child to speak, it's not helpful.

- Listen carefully to your child. He may be saying more than you think. Remember what you've asked him, even if it was a few minutes before. The answer might pop out!
- The four key language skills are: vocabulary, clarity of speech, sentence length, and conversational give-and-take.
- Show your child the power of his language by being responsive when he says something to you, especially if it's a new word or sentence.
- Go directly for language instead of using message boards, flash cards, etc.
- If your child is echoing what you are saying, treat this language literally.
- When your child wants you to do something for her, ask her for a word (or words) that are one step beyond what she has mastered.
- Don't forget how important eye contact is!
- Take your time. You don't have to remember everything. Try putting some of this into practice and see how it goes. Add more as you go along.

#10

Make Sure Food Isn't Part of the Problem

You are what you eat?

Terrance

Many years ago, a family came from England for a two-week stay at ATCA. Their son, Terrance, didn't speak and had many stims. He also had an unusual diet: he only ate chocolate-covered cookies that were in the shape of Elmo from *Sesame Street*.

When I say he only ate those cookies, I mean it literally. There was nothing else in little Terrance's diet except the cookies. His family, knowing that they'd be in the States for two weeks, brought several packages of the cookies with them. This was smart, as they were not available in America at the time.

It was an interesting situation. We had never seen someone who only ate cookies. The staff had discussions about how he was able to get enough nutrition from the cookies to live. We figured he was just barely getting enough to survive.

Terrance was very thin. There were dark circles under his eyes and he was very pale. Still, he ate his cookies. The staff encouraged him to eat vegetables and fruits, but Terrance knew his Elmo cookies were close by and saw no reason to eat anything besides his favorite (and only) food.

However, there was something Terrance's parents had not planned for: at ATCA, children work harder than normal and generally burn up a lot more energy. This means they usually eat a lot more food.

Terrance ran out of chocolate-covered Elmo cookies on the first Thursday afternoon (the fourth day). This presented a real problem for his family. There were no more cookies left in the apartment, and, worse, none in the eastern hemisphere! The staff was thrilled about the possibility of offering Terrance healthier foods without the Elmo cookies looming over us, making our excited and fun suggestions to eat broccoli all but meaningless.

I was the first person into the room on day five (Friday). I brought a bowl of oatmeal and a spoon into the room with me. Terrance had been sitting, playing with stuffed animals when he looked up and saw me.

Suddenly screaming, Terrance ran at me, took the bowl of oatmeal, threw it into the bathroom, and slammed the bathroom door. For a moment, he stood quietly, looking at me. Then he screamed again and ran back to his stuffed animal.

I put down the spoon and got a stuffed animal of my own to play with. After a little bit of time, we began to play together. Sometimes he would stim and I would join him, sometimes he would look up and I would tickle him...it was normal stuff for the ATCA playroom.

After forty-five minutes, I opened the bathroom door. There was a new bowl of oatmeal sitting on the sink. Someone had observed Terrance throwing the first bowl and brought another for me to offer him. (The bathroom had a second door to the observation room, so food was often delivered this way.)

Déjà vu! Terrance spied the new bowl of oatmeal, ran screaming at me, grabbed the bowl, threw it in the bathroom, and slammed the door.

This series of events repeated itself several times throughout the day with different members of the staff and all different types of foods.

Saturday morning, day six, I entered the room with another bowl of oatmeal. It was a new day, and I was hopeful that Terrance had adjusted to the new situation.

He had, slightly. When I walked in, he allowed me to bring the oatmeal into the room. He did not scream or throw it in the bathroom. Progress!

Terrance was on one side of the playroom, fiddling with a toy truck. I was on the other side of the room with the bowl of oatmeal. In an attempt to model how enjoyable eating oatmeal could be, I scooped some onto the spoon and brought it up to my mouth. Suddenly there was screaming. Terrance came to me, grabbed the bowl of oatmeal, threw it into the bathroom, and slammed the door.

I still saw this as progress. On Friday, I couldn't even bring the bowl into the room, and only one day later he allowed me to do that (admittedly with the condition that no one eat from the bowl—but still, it was movement).

I played with him for thirty minutes. Then, I got a new bowl of oatmeal, and the process repeated itself.

The third time I did this, Terrance did not throw the bowl into the bathroom or scream. He just kept playing with his truck. He allowed me to eat the oatmeal as I sat on the other side of the room.

More progress! Over the course of the day, Terrance eventually allowed the staff to bring all sorts of foods near him (although there were several times he screamed and threw the food into the bathroom). He got used to foods being in his life.

I said in a staff meeting that it was the worst eating disorder I've ever seen. All we could do was show him that the Elmo cookies weren't coming, no matter how long he held out, and present other options to him.

On Sunday he took a cautious bite of oatmeal. Then, suddenly, he ate several bowls of it. I'm sure he was very hungry.

Over the course of his time at ATCA, Terrance ate oatmeal, bananas, crackers, and bread. He developed a fondness for foods that were lightly colored. And his family never had to feed him chocolate-covered Elmo cookies again.

Problem Foods

Many autistic children eat a very limited diet. Here's a list of foods that many will eat:
- Food from McDonald's or Burger King
- Cookies
- Ice cream
- Candy
- Pizza
- Bread
- Soda
- Milk
- White sugar (I remember one boy who I worked with in Puerto Rico who would find the sugar wherever his mother hid it and eat it in

handfuls as fast as he could. It was like watching a crack addict.)

There are certainly more, but that's a quick selection for you. Interestingly enough, each of these foods may cause problems for your child if he eats it (yes, even milk and bread).

Of course, most children won't touch the types of foods that will help them grow and learn optimally: fruits and vegetables.

The Problem with Sugar

Many children with autism do not regulate their energy well. They are often hyperactive, lethargic, or both. Giving your child foods with sugar in them is giving your child's body more energy than it can process effectively. With all this energy, it will be hard for your child to concentrate on the things you care about, like eye contact and language.

This doesn't mean you have to completely remove sugar from your child's diet, though some people would recommend it. The more regulated your child is, the easier it will be for him to learn the things you want him to learn.

Intolerances: Bread and Dairy

Many parents report that their children have an intolerance of dairy products. This is not the dairy itself, but the primary protein in dairy, which is called casein.

Children who have dairy intolerances often show remarkable changes once they have avoided dairy for several months. It is not that unusual for a family to tell me that their child started speaking once they removed dairy products from his diet. Or improved eye contact. Or attention span. Or a number of other skills.

This same theory also applies to breads. The primary protein in wheat is called gluten. Many parents report that their children have an intolerance of gluten.

There are substitutes for both dairy products and breads on the market. Soy products actually taste pretty good, though most of the bread products are a little, well, not so tasty.

There are many labs that test for these intolerances. It is relatively inexpensive and you can do the test by mail.

What He's Really Eating

Here's a chart to help you understand what your child is eating. Make a list of the foods your child eats the most. Note if the food is high in sugar, dairy, or bread.

What My Child Is Eating

Food	Sugar	Dairy	Bread
Chocolate milk	Yes	Yes	No

Look over the chart. How much does your child eat sugar, dairy, and bread? If your child is typical of autistic children, the answer will most likely be "a lot."

If your child is eating lots of these foods, changing his diet will probably help him learn skills faster.

Presentation: How Foods Look

The kinds of foods your child should be eating are fruits and vegetables. I know, I know—she won't eat fruits and vegetables. But that's because she has trained you not to offer them to her (or trained you to give up very quickly on the healthy foods and give her the McNuggets).

There are two things you have to do to help your child eat healthier foods: take away the unhealthy foods and focus on presentation.

We've already discussed removing unhealthy foods. Remember, you have to take them away and keep them away! Most kids know that you will give in long before they do. You have to be more persistent than your child or else you *will* lose this one.

By presentation, I mean both making the foods appear interesting and presenting them with determination and optimism.

Here are some ways you can make vegetables appear different and possibly interesting:
- Mash them
- Cut them into shapes that your child enjoys, like Big Bird or letters or five-pointed stars

- Steam them
- Boil them
- Julienne them
- Add food coloring so you can serve blue carrots
- Serve on a tiny plate
- Serve on a huge plate
- Serve in a mug or glass
- You eat the vegetables, show how much you like them, then offer them to your child

There are potentially hundreds more ways to present foods to your child. Think about what he is motivated by and try to use that motivation in the presentation. For example, if he likes the *Toy Story* movies, feed the vegetables to Buzz Lightyear before you offer them to him.

Presentation: Your Determination and Optimism

Your child can tell what you think about the foods you offer to him. If you hate broccoli, then it's going to be hard for you to encourage your child to eat it. You have to decide that you love broccoli, or only offer him fruits and veggies that you do enjoy.

One time during an intensive program, a family wanted to change their child's diet. He had only been eating foods with sugar. We chopped up some carrots and gave them to his mother. She looked at me warily and said, "Patrick's not going to eat these."

"Just try," I said. She nodded and went in the room with the carrots.

She played with her son for about ten minutes until finally she pulled a carrot out of the bowl and said, "Do you want...one of these?"

She said this with little enthusiasm and with a look of concern on her face. Patrick barely looked at the carrot, but did push it away lightly with his hand.

"Okay," she said and put the carrot away. She did not offer him carrots again for the rest of her session.

When it was time for her to leave the room, one of our staff members went in to work with Patrick. His mother and I observed the work through the viewing window. The staff member played with Patrick a little, and then, making sounds reminiscent of the Six Million Dollar Man running, pulled out a carrot in slow motion. Patrick watched, interested. Then, still making the "ruh-ruh-ruh" sounds, the staff member slowly fed the carrot to a teddy bear. Patrick smiled.

Then, the staff member, still making the sounds and moving in slow motion, brought a carrot to Patrick's mouth. Patrick took a bite, and then another.

He ate the entire carrot. Then he ate the whole bowl of carrots.

Patrick's mother looked at me and said, "I didn't think that was possible."

You have to believe your child is going to eat the carrots. If you buy into this, you will be more persistent, more creative, and just more fun when you offer the food.

When you combine taking away unhealthy foods (so there are no other options), making the foods look interesting and different, and your own optimism and determination, it creates a situation where your child will, over time, become motivated to eat foods he is not currently eating.

To Review:

- What your child eats matters.
- Some children with autism have intolerances of dairy and/or wheat. You can get your child tested for this.
- Even if there is no intolerance, most kids eat way too much sugar and other foods that interfere with their development.
- The way to change your child's diet is to remove the offending foods entirely and show your child that they are not coming back.

- Your child will eat when he's hungry.
- How you present the new foods to your child makes a huge difference!

Conclusion

So those are the 10 things you can do right now to help your child with autism. It's okay if you do one, or three, or five, or all of them. No pressure. This book is intended to be a tool for you to help your child develop in the most meaningful ways possible.

It's not easy being the parent of a child with autism. There are so many times when you just don't know what to do, or feel angry, sad, or guilty about the situation. Underneath it all, even if you haven't done everything perfectly, the love you have for your child is what will fuel you, and what makes the biggest difference of all to your child's continued growth.

To all the parents, brothers, sisters, aunts, uncles, grandparents, teachers, friends, and professionals: I salute your dedication and caring for your very special child.

Appendix

10 Things Seminar

Ready to learn more? Do you want to see these techniques in action? Go to TenThingsAutism.com and check out our online courses today.

Author Jonathan Levy presents a series of online workshops that will show you how to put the "Ten Things" directly into practice.

Watch as Jonathan Levy demonstrates the "Ten Things."
Listen as he explains each technique in detail.
Learn how to be more effective with your child.

www.TenThingsAutism.com

Index

child reaction, 103–105
example, 52
exiting, desire, 103–105
issues, 105
reactions, 104
stimming, increase, 103
Looking up, eye strain, 21
Looks
celebration, 23, 26
duration/spontaneity, 20
number, chart, 19

M
McDonald's food, problems, 155
Milk, problems, 155
Motivating factors, 5
Motivation. *See* Child motivation
discomfort. *See* Self-motivation
Movement, speed (attentiveness), 81
Multi-word sentences, usage, 138

N
New people, child reaction (example), 8–9
No, usage/impact, 93
Non-autistic children, impact.
See Classroom
Nonchalance
reaction, 7
usage, 5
Non-distracting room
advice, 105–106
arrangement, 101
impact. *See* Stims
one-on-one interaction, 91
review, 106–107
Nonreaction. *See* Enthusiasm
learning, 7
Nonverbal behavior, 13
Nonverbal communication, 81
reliance, 131
Normal face, 116

O
One-on-one interaction. *See*
Non-distracting room
involvement, 100–102
One-word sentences, usage, 138
Outdoors, environment, 93
Overdescription, problem. *See* Speech
Overstimulation, 92
withdrawal, 34

P
Parenting, teaching, 10
Parents, response (impact), 6
Partner, face (examination), 116
People
attitude. *See* Child behavior
child interaction, 94
ability, 43
Permission, obtaining, 72
Physical interaction, change, 69
Physical manipulation
definition, 67–69
examples, 68
necessity, 72–74
Physical needs, satisfaction, 33
Physical stims, 31–32
Pizza, problems, 155
Playroom
entry, enticement, 66
example, 154
Police restraint, physical manipulation, 67
Positioning, importance. *See* Eye contact
Problem foods, 151
cookie example, 151–155
review, 162–163
Pronouns, improvement, 138
Pronunciation
focus, absence, 122
habits, teaching, 123
impact, 128
improvement, 130
quality, absence, 129